T. J. COLES was awarded a PhD for work on the aesthetic experiences of blind and visually impaired people. His thesis, *The Knotweed Factor*, draws on the philosophy underpinning cognitive psychology and neurological approaches to blindness. (It can be read online.) A columnist with Axis of Logic, Coles has written a number of political books, including *Britain's Secret Wars*, *The Great Brexit Swindle* and *President Trump, Inc.* and edited the anthology *Voices for Peace*. He was shortlisted for the Martha Gellhorn Prize (2013) for a series of articles about Libya.

FIRE AND FURY

HOW THE US ISOLATES NORTH KOREA, ENCIRCLES CHINA AND RISKS NUCLEAR WAR IN ASIA

T. J. COLES

CLAIRVIEW

Clairview Books Ltd.,
Russet, Sandy Lane,
West Hoathly,
W. Sussex RH19 4QQ

www.clairviewbooks.com

Published in Great Britain in 2017 by Clairview Books

A CIP catalogue record for this book is available from the British Library

Print book ISBN 978 1 905570 93 5
Ebook ISBN 978 1 905570 94 2

Cover by Morgan Creative. Statue of Liberty portrait © Pineapples
Typeset by DP Photosetting, Neath, West Glamorgan
Printed and bound by 4Edge Ltd, Essex

'U.S. war-gaming consistently predicts at least one million casualties on both sides...'

Cato Institute (in reference to a
North Korea–South Korea/US war)

Contents

Acronyms   ix

Introduction   1

1. The US and China   6
  'Full-spectrum dominance' and the importance
     of oil   6
  The Asia Pivot: 'Shape the region's rules and
     norms'   10
  Japan and the Peace Constitution: 'The Japanese
  people still don't understand'   13
  US–China relations: 'Challenges to the
     US-dominated order'   16
  China–North Korea relations: 'Emphasizing
     economic development'   20
  The US–China–NK axis: 'China's greatest concern
     is reserved for the US military presence'   25

2. The US and North Korea   29
  Genocidal rhetoric: North Korea's 'extinction'   29
  Korea: historical background: 'Anti-colonial struggle'   31
  North–South: partition and war: 'We burned down
     every town in North Korea'   31
  North Korea: the Cold War and after: 'Stiffening
     quills, retreating into its shell'   38

3. North Korea and the Rest of the World   42
  North Korea–South Korea: 'The Vietnam war
     caused NK to act when it did'   42

NK–Japanese relations: 'North Korea cannot survive
without food and oil'   53
Russia–North Korea: 'Economic relations
expanded alarmingly'   56
North Korea's economy: Moving towards 'free
markets'?   58
Pipeline politics: 'Peace pipelines'   60

4. **Fantasy vs. Facts**   64
Nuclear weapons, missiles and posture: 'War could
erupt from a simple miscalculation'   64
The threat: Image and reality: 'Deterring foreign
enemies'   72
North Korea's diplomacy: 'Axis of evil'   77
Sanctions: 'Food aid has fallen due to sanctions'   86
Provocations: 'We have no authority to seize cargo'   89

Conclusion: What can we do?   92

Notes   99

Index   114

Acronyms

4D	Detect, disrupt, destroy and defend
ABM	Antiballistic Missile
BMD	Ballistic Missile 'Defense'
CFR	Council on Foreign Relations
CIA	Central Intelligence Agency
DMZ	Demilitarized Zone
DoD	Department of Defense
DPRK	Democratic People's Republic of Korea (North Korea)
FAO	Food and Agricultural Organization
GDP	Gross Domestic Product
GSOMIA	General security of military information agreement
IAEA	International Atomic Energy Agency
ICBM	Intercontinental Ballistic Missile
KIC	Kaesong Industrial Complex
LNG	Liquefied Natural Gas
MoD	Ministry of Defence
NATO	North Atlantic Treaty Organization
NGO	Nongovernmental organization
NK	North Korea
NLL	Northern Limit Line
NPT	Nuclear Non-Proliferation Treaty
OECD	Organization for Economic Cooperation and Development
OPLAN	Operations Plan
PNAC	Project for the New American Century
ROK	Republic of Korea (South Korea)

SDN	Special Designated Nationals
SIPRI	Stockholm International Peace Research Institute
SK	South Korea
SPARK	Solidarity for Peace and Reunification of Korea
THAAD	Theater High Altitude Area Defense
UN	United Nations
UNC	United Nations Command–South Korea
UNICEF	United Nations Children's Fund
UNSCR	UN Security Council Resolution
USSR	Union of Soviet Socialist Republics
WFP	World Food Programme

Introduction

This book is about US military hegemony in Asia. Crucially, it is about the *response* of Asian countries, particularly North Korea, to this threat. The mainstream and to a large extent alternative media in the West omit America's regional provocations and only report North Korea's retaliations and responses. To Western audiences, North Korea seems like a genuine threat and a regime out of control. But US military threat assessments and strategic analysts paint quite a different picture.

Despite what some readers will claim, this book is not apologia for the North Korean regime. People who make baseless allegations that a person is an apologist for foreign regimes are usually themselves apologists for Western imperialism because they believe in violence as the primary method of resolving global issues and in the mythology perpetuated by their state about its own supposed greatness. The NK regime is despicable and if North Koreans want it reformed or dismantled, we should use peaceful means to help them; as long as the consequences are not worse for ordinary North Koreans. The signs are already there that the regime is reforming. It is introducing a market economy (for better or worse) and trying to extend diplomatic relations with China and Russia. The US is seeking to isolate it.

If we are concerned with helping people living under oppression, we might start with ending ties to close allies who are as bad if not worse than the North Korean regime: the Saudi establishment, for instance. Next, we might put pressure on our own Western governments not to keep North

Korea isolated. Western media have inverted this and claim that North Korea lives in self-imposed isolation.

The points laid out in this Introduction are backed-up throughout the book in endnotes, most of which come from establishment sources, such as the US Congressional Research Service and even the Pentagon. It is striking to compare the governmental and military record to the mainstream and even alternative media's version of events concerning North Korea and China. The policy of America's strategic elite is extremely dangerous. Several strategic analysts quoted later warn that nuclear weapons could be fired in error. This could lead to the end of life as we know it, and possibly put an end to all life.

Taking an evidence-based approach, this book proves that what we are taught about North Korea in Western media is largely false. In reality:

1) North Korea is not globally isolated. It has diplomatic relations with over 100 countries, but more needs to be done to assist its integration.
2) It has not sought self-imposed isolation or hermitage. Rather, the United States has sought to isolate it for political reasons, which will be explained.
3) North Korea is not a global threat because its global strike capacity is not only limited but highly exaggerated by the regime.
4) North Korea has repeatedly made efforts and offers to negotiate with the USA and regional powers and has been rejected or undermined on each occasion.
5) America's North Korea policy is ambiguous: as far as elite US planners are concerned, there are pros and cons to keeping the regime alive.

A much bigger long-term interest for the USA is China. This book argues that the overarching regional goal of US military planners and transnational corporations is to contain China. In order to contain something, the given thing has to be expanding. So, where is China expanding? China is building regional military bases on disputed islands and is building a single military base in Djibouti, Africa. That's it. The real 'containment' of China is an ideological one: to make sure than China continues to act as an assembly plant for US products, keeps its markets open to US corporations and most importantly does not interfere economically or geo-politically with US strategic interests.

The USA, on the other hand, is engaged in seven open wars, an unknown number of covert operations, has over 600 mili-tary bases around the world and is committed to a military doctrine called Full Spectrum Dominance. Its war planners and policymakers are driven by the usual ideology: that America is uniquely great and that so-called free-market capitalism is the best economic system to impose upon the world in order to ensure prosperity and even security. (In the real world, this is the best system to ensure that wealth is accrued by the few and that fewer than 200 US corporations control 40% of global trade and investment.) As we shall see in this book, recent US military assessments confirm that China has no aspirations of becoming a global or even regional superpower, and that even if China wanted to, it lacks the military capacity.

In the region sits a nuclear-armed Russia, which, like China, retains some state controls over its economy, hence the constant demonization of Russia in Western media. The US is putting pressure on its regional allies, the non-nuclear-armed Japan and South Korea, in order to continue threat-ening China.

In the middle of this potentially explosive situation sits North Korea.

As this book examines, US policy toward North Korea is complicated. On the one hand, the US wants the regime to collapse so that a client regime can take its place. A client regime in North Korea would be hostile to neighbouring China and Russia. In this respect, a replacement client regime would act as a US proxy.

This would block the long-proposed Russia–South Korea pipeline, which is planned to run through North Korea and provide South Korea with Russian energy and a port to export energy across the high seas. The US and Britain have already partially blocked Russia's energy route to Europe by sponsoring coups and a civil war in Ukraine. A similar scenario could play out in Korea. By expanding military ties with India and continuing its occupation of Afghanistan, the US has already made indirect threats against China. With a client regime in North Korea, the threat could be even more real.

On the other hand, the US does not want the North Korean regime to collapse. It wants it to survive; the reason being that as soon as the North Korean regime collapses, the pretexts for basing tens of thousands of US forces in South Korea vanishes. The US has a significant presence in South Korea, which is only marginally designed to repel an invasion from North Korea. A second reason for the US wanting the regime to survive is the fear that a progressive government could come to power. Such a government could use the country's resources, such as its uranium mines and rare-earth metals, to benefit its people. Such a government would also forge alliances with left-wing elements in the South and even Japan. The US could rapidly lose political control.

For the USA, the best of both worlds is a regime that keeps up the dangerous rhetoric but is a secret ally with the US and its regional partners. This way, US military systems can continue to be aimed at China under the pretext of countering North Korea, while the North opens 'free markets' and accepts US economic penetration.

1

The US and China

'Full-spectrum dominance' and the importance of oil
In 1997, the US Space Command announced its intention to rule the world by force via a doctrine called Full Spectrum Dominance, which involves securing land, sea, air, space and information, 'to protect US national interests and investment'. Rebecca Johnson of the UN Disarmament Commission commented: '[n]otions of full spectrum dominance ... are perceived as a security threat by countries that have no political desire or intention to threaten the United States, but which would be expected by their own citizens and militaries to develop countermeasures to deter the United States nevertheless'.[1]

At the time, the only rival superpower, the Soviet Union, had collapsed leaving the US free to dominate regions that it could not have in the presence of the nuclear-armed USSR. The Middle East, where most of the world's oil is, became the prime target for direct occupation. In the 1960s, America's Central Intelligence Agency was concerned that the USSR could control 7% of the international oil market. 'This will enable the Soviet Union to upset markets in various individual consuming countries and even displace Western companies in smaller markets.' Soviet petrodollars could 'make the USSR a force to be reckoned with in the international petroleum field'. The CIA worried that an 'influx of Soviet oil is likely ... to spur further price cuts with a consequent disrupting influence on relations between the Middle Eastern governments and the Western companies'.[2]

Unlike Russia, China is not self-sufficient in energy. The US has targeted China's potential energy assets in various theatres. The following information does not infer that hegemony over China was the sole policy issue for the US, but nevertheless it was certainly a key consequence.

Iraq has the second largest oil reserves in the Middle East. By sanctioning Iraq for 13 years (and killing a million Iraqis, mostly children, in the process) Britain and the US kept China from affordable Iraqi oil. The US and Britain invaded Iraq in 2003 and built permanent military bases. When international corporations were permitted to bid to steal Iraq's oil, Iraqi auctioneers set too high a price, forcing China to reject the price offers. By helping to create a permanent state of war in Iraq (most recently with the growth of Daesh), Iraq's oil is too unstable for international corporations to purchase at a decent and predictable price.[3]

Iran has the third largest oil reserves in the Middle East after Saudi Arabia and Iraq. Iran could build pipelines to carry oil and gas to China through their neighbour Afghanistan. Iran could also carry oil and gas to India through their neighbour Pakistan. By occupying Afghanistan on a permanent basis, the US and Britain not only encircle both Iran and China with military bases, they prevent the possibility of an Iran–China-friendly government from forming in Afghanistan. Crucially, they prevent pipelines from being built.[4]

Libya has the largest oil reserves in Africa. By training and arming Islamic extremists to overthrow the stable regime of Muammar Gaddafi, the US, Britain and France pushed out the thousands of Chinese oil, gas and engineering contractors working in the country. After NATO smashed up Libya, killing 50,000 people (according to the puppet regime installed by the US, Britain and France), Libya's oil economy under factions of Islamic extremists has become almost as unpredictable as Iraq's under Daesh.[5]

Sudan also had some of the largest oil deposits in Africa. Under the Bashir regime, China had lucrative contracts. In the early 2000s, the US led the agenda to bring Western media attention to Darfur, where Sudanese government-linked militia were committing atrocities against civilians. The US-led sanctions on Sudan hurt China's oil interests. The US also helped engineer the split in Sudan, roughly along Christian–Muslim lines. This created the new country of South Sudan, which happens to have most of the former country's oil reserves. In sum, China ended up allied to an oil-poor North and the US allied with an oil-rich South.[6]

In Somalia, the US and Britain trained and organized the terrorist government (the Transitional Federal Government, TFG) to overthrow what the US State Department describes as the non-extremist, socialistic Islamic Courts Union. This led to what journalist Aidan Hartley described as a 'manmade' famine, which killed tens of thousands of people. It also led to a refugee crisis between 2007 and 2009, in which millions of Somalis fled to Yemen, Kenya and other parts of Somalia to avoid the TFG. The decimation of Somalia had the effect of terminating Russian and Chinese oil contracts in the country.[7]

Finally, in Zimbabwe the US and Britain turned against their former ally Robert Mugabe (whose forces the UK had once trained), suddenly realizing that he is a dictator. The sanctions imposed on the fragile Zimbabwean economy helped send the currency into a spiral of unprecedented inflation. This had predictable effects, also seen in Sudan and Somalia: lowered life expectancy, increased infant mortality and general misery and hopelessness. Chinese oil contractors were compelled to abandon many of their operations.[8]

In 2008, the *New York Times* expressed euphoria that this policy of 'containment' seemed to work:

> Beijing has been quietly overhauling its policies toward pariah states. It strongly denounced North Korea's nuclear test in October 2006 and took the lead, with the United States, in drafting a sweeping United Nations sanctions resolution against Pyongyang. Over the past year, it has voted to impose and then tighten sanctions on Iran, it has supported the deployment of a United Nations–African Union (UN–AU) force in Darfur, and it has condemned a brutal government crackdown in Burma (which the ruling junta renamed Myanmar in 1989). China is now willing to condition its diplomatic protection of pariah countries, forcing them to become more acceptable to the international community.[9]

'International community' means the USA and its allies.

In addition to choking China's access to oil and gas, the US has devised a long-range strategy for intensifying military operations in the Asia Pacific. A report by the Oxford Institute for Energy Studies states:

> Rising volumes of crude purchases represent a heavy financial toll on state coffers, while the risk of a supply cut-off, mainly by China's strategic rival, the US, has been a growing preoccupation. Chinese officials have been worried about the US's naval supremacy and its de facto dominance of key strategic trade points, especially the Straits of Malacca – through which around 85% of China's own commodity imports transit.[10]

The so-called Asia Pivot (documented in the next section) has historical roots.

In the year 2000, the George W. Bush circle of so-called neocons published a strategy paper for their now-defunct Project for the New American Century. Sponsored by the arms industry and former-future political elites, the document states (referring to the Gulf War and US–British sanctions on Iraq): 'While the unresolved conflict with Iraq provides the immediate justification, the need for a substantial American force presence in the Gulf transcends the issue of the regime of Saddam Hussein'; hence the lies about Saddam being linked to 9/11 and having a weapons of mass destruction pro-gramme. The PNAC authors were horrified that Clinton initiated the Comprehensive Test Ban Treaty, for reasons they explain: 'Rather than maintain and improve America's nuclear deterrent', meaning offensive strike capabilities, 'Clinton … put his faith in new arms control measures'. The neocons express their deep concern that peace treaties 'would … constrain America's unique role in providing the global nuclear umbrella that helps to keep states like Japan and South Korea from developing [nuclear] weapons'.[11]

PNAC goes on to note that '[i]f the United States is to remain the guarantor of security in Northeast Asia, and to hold together a de facto alliance whose other main pillars are Korea and Japan maintaining forward-based U.S. forces is essential'. Security means regional dominance. This domi-nance is a threat to the security of all peoples in the region, as most Koreans in the North and South understand.[12]

The Asia Pivot: 'Shape the region's rules and norms'
The PNAC document goes on to advocate developing THAAD missiles, engaging in global 'constabulary missions', revoking

the Anti-Ballistic Missile Treaty (1972) with Russia, using US drones to project US power globally and funding a hi-tech army of soldiers bolstered by chemical additives. This cannot happen quickly without a 'catastrophic and catalyzing event', the authors explain. Enter 9/11.[13]

US attention briefly shifted from Asia and centred on the Middle East and Central Asia. As part of the so-called 'war on terror', the US and Britain invaded and/or attacked Afghanistan (2001, occupation), Yemen (2002, drones), Iraq (2003, occupation), Pakistan (2004, drones), Somalia (2006, missiles), Libya (2011, via NATO and proxies) and Syria (2011, with proxies, later drones). The US-based Physicians for Social Responsibility estimates that the wars in Afghanistan, Iraq and Pakistan alone killed 1.3 million people.[14]

Now the USA had more influence in the oil-rich Middle East, with its permanent bases in Saudi Arabia, Iraq and Afghanistan, plus its encirclement of Iran, it set about expanding military forces across Asia, where crucial shipping lanes intersect.

Not long after he entered office, Barack Obama raised US military spending to record levels and authorized the so-called 'pivot to Asia', which means the intimidation of China. In 2011, US Secretary of State Hillary Clinton falsely claimed that the wars in Afghanistan and Iraq were winding down (in fact, they were entering a new phase with the rise of Daesh and new excuses for US intervention). But America's hegemony would not end there. 'In the next ten years, we need to be smart and systematic about where we invest our time and energy', Clinton explained. 'One of the most important tasks of American statecraft over the next decade will ... be to lock in a substantially increased investment – diplomatic, economic, strategic, and otherwise – in the Asia–Pacific region'.[15]

Financially, this means maintaining flows of US foreign direct investment. Diplomatically, it means fostering a regional investment treaty (the Trans-Pacific Partnership, which the US got several countries to sign and then backed out of), and militarily it means building the regional component of Full Spectrum Dominance, namely the Asia Pivot. 'U.S. commitment there is essential', said Clinton. Clinton likens potential investment in the region to US imperial ambitions in WWII. She refers to the US as a 'Pacific power'. The objectives include 'keeping the sea lanes free for commerce and navigation', for US business interests. '[O]ur work abroad holds the key to our prosperity and security at home.' Clinton was addressing her major constituents, the US business sector. Another objective is to use the presence of America's military to keep markets conducive to US interests and ensure that pesky nationalism doesn't take hold. 'Open markets in Asia provide the United States with unprecedented opportunities for investment, trade, and access to cutting-edge technology', like its smartphones built in near slave-labour conditions in Chinese factories.[16]

Several factors stand in the way of uncontrolled US dominance: 1) Russia, 2) China, 3) North Korea's possession of nuclear weapons, and 4) the peoples of the region, including South Koreans and Japanese, who put pressure on domestic governments to withdraw support for US military bases in the region.

The US Congressional Research Service has lengthy reports on the so-called Asia Pivot, one of which suggests that it is better to pursue the policy of domination than risk other countries (especially Russia and China) shaping the region in ways unfavourable to US commercial interests. '[M]any would argue that the potential costs of *inaction* arguably could outweigh the risks of action' (emphasis in original). Three nuclear powers – China, North Korea and Russia – will respond and are responding to US military expansion in the region. It is a chilling insight into the psychology of US war planners and policymakers who would rather risk nuclear confrontation or accident than abandon a region and allow it to develop independent of US influence.[17]

Although the Pivot started off with a small case, with a modest troop increase, it was 'designed to have a large *symbolic* impact', says the CRS report; namely intimidating regional powers (emphasis in original). 'Administration officials argue that demonstrating a lasting U.S. commitment to Asia will make bilateral partners and Asian multilateral organizations more willing and able to shape the region's rules and norms collectively'. The CRS report also notes that the Asia Pivot is designed 'to encourage constructive Chinese behavior'.[18]

The US government's US–China Economic and Security Commission (2016) states: 'China perceives U.S. policy on North Korea is designed to strengthen U.S. alliances with South Korea and Japan, which it views are being leveraged to contain China'. The report also notes that 'the recent decision by South Korea and the United States to deploy a THAAD ballistic missile defense system battalion in South Korea appears to be reinforcing Beijing's long-held suspicion of U.S. intentions on the Korean Peninsula'.[19]

Japan and the Peace Constitution: 'The Japanese people still don't understand'

America's renewed 'defence' deal with Japan is primarily aimed at containing China's regional ambitions, thereby ensuring US freedom of action. Following decades of dedicated protest by Japanese civilians over the presence of US military bases in their country, thousands rally against moves by the Abe government to alter Japan's 'Peace Constitution' and prepare to engage in overseas military operations.

In WWII, the US killed three million Japanese (mostly with incendiary bombing) and destroyed 70% of the country, before dropping two nuclear weapons (on Hiroshima and Nagasaki). The country was in no position to do anything but accept US demands, including accepting a 'Peace Constitution', which prohibits Japan from using its military abroad.

The move announced in July 2015 follows the Guidelines for US–Japan Defense Cooperation (GDC). The US-drafted GDC is enacted 'to ensure Japan's peace and security under any circumstances', a phrase so broad as to infer that any Chinese defensive measure could be met with military force, giving the US and Japan *carte blanche* to operate in the region. It continues: the US will 'extend deterrence to Japan through the full range of capabilities, including U.S. nuclear forces. The United States also will continue to forward deploy combat-ready forces in the Asia–Pacific region and maintain the ability to reinforce those forces rapidly'.[20]

Responding to the renewal of GDC, Chinese Foreign Ministry spokesman Hong Lei said: 'The U.S.–Japan alliance is a bilateral arrangement forged during the Cold War period ... [T]he Cold War is long-gone'. US actions are heating it up. The Chinese Ministry of Defence said: '[the] military alliance is an outdated product which goes against the trends of times featuring peace, development, cooperation and mutual benefit'.[21]

Since 2008, Russia and China have repeatedly introduced treaties to the United Nations in an effort to prohibit cyber-war and space weaponization. The treaties were rejected by the US. In keeping with the Full Spectrum Dominance doctrine, US spokeswoman Dana Perino explained: 'The United States opposes the development of new legal regimes or other restrictions that seek to prohibit or limit access to or use of space'. A year later, the US rejected a Russian–Chinese proposal to ban cyberwarfare. The *New York Times* put it simply: 'The United States argues that a treaty is unnecessary'.[22]

As China proposed peace treaties, the US expanded. A paper written for the US Center for Strategic and International Studies notes that the Asia Pivot strategy 'has prompted Chinese anxiety about U.S. containment and heightened regional worries about intensified U.S.–China strategic competition'. The paper followed a US intelligence report to Congress which confirms that China – which spends onetenth as much on its military as the US – is not an international threat.[23]

In 2015, the US Defense Department – in sharp contrast to media reporting – confirmed China's interest in normalizing relations with the US: 'China seeks to ensure basic stability along its periphery and avoid direct confrontation with the United States in order to focus on domestic development and smooth China's rise'. It notes that '[l]imited logistical support remains a key obstacle preventing the PLA [People's Liberation Army of China's] Navy from operating more extensively beyond East Asia, particularly in the Indian Ocean'.[24]

The report concludes that 'China remains far behind the United States ... [in] resisting electronic attack and the capacity to respond to multiple warheads. Finally, if China is to deploy an effective BMD [Ballistic Missile Defence] system, it will need to be supported by a space-based early warning system, currently missing from China's BMD infrastructure'.[25]

According to the GDC noted above, massive surveillance – including BMD – is part of the US–Japan deal.

The people of Japan have responded to growing US–Japanese collaboration by increasing their protests against US militarism. According to the BBC (with its usual spin), '[s]everal recent polls showed that more than half of Japanese voters were opposed to passing the bills' to end the Peace Constitution. Expressing his contempt for the public, Prime Minister Abe said: 'Unfortunately, the Japanese people still don't have a substantial understanding ... I will work harder so public understanding would deepen'.[26]

One hundred thousand civilians protested outside the Assembly to oppose the Lower House's passing of the bill. 'The protest was reminiscent of those that toppled Prime Minister Shinzo Abe's grandfather from the premiership 55 years ago after he rammed a revised US–Japan security pact through parliament', says Reuters. 'Many' of the protestors 'stayed well into the night, chanting and holding up placards reading "Abe, quit", "No War, No Killing" and "Scrap the War Bills" '.[27]

US–China relations: 'Challenges to the US-dominated order'

Even before the US entered WWII, winning it and thus dominating much of the world, it coveted Japan's regional empire. The US Congressional Research Service explains that '[m]any aspects of the "Pacific Pivot" ' announced by Obama in 2011, 'represent an expansion rather than a transformation of U.S. policy'. Obama, the authors explain, merely followed 'a long line of U.S. governments' and their interest in Asia.[28]

'China's rise thus far has already bred geopolitical, military, economic, and ideological challenges to ... the U.S.-dominated international order', write two authors for the business-government-linked US Council on Foreign Relations (CFR). China has to fail, say the authors. 'Its continued, even if uneven, success in the future would further undermine U.S. national interests'. Until recently, China was the 'workshop of the world'. But more recently, '[t]his economic model of production for overseas markets is slowly changing' and is thus a threat to the USA, whose business class profits from cheap Chinese labour. The authors note that 'state capitalism' is portrayed by China's leadership as a 'superior alternative to the American framework of free markets'.[29]

To put it simply, the US worked hard to persuade China's political elites to adopt 'free markets'. Doing so boosted China's GDP (to the benefit of the country's financial elites) and also its military spending. Increased economic prosperity in China's financial sector was of huge benefit to US financial institutions and its newly opened labour markets were of benefit to US tech firms. China had enough financial and thus military clout to pose a challenge of sorts to US interests in the region and perhaps follow an independent course. This is called the 'Asia paradox' in international relations.[30]

One of the problems for the USA posed by a growing China is that other countries in the region (e.g., Vietnam) have become less dependent on the US and more 'dependent on China'. The US planners want every country in the region dependent on the USA, not China. This has 'produced several unnerving strategic consequences', say the CFR authors. Another of which is the possibility that US allies will switch their allegiances to China and look to its growing military and nuclear arsenal for protection. Finally, China has 'undermine[d] the standards of governance set by the [OECD], the

World Bank and other international institutions', led by the USA, by forming Cooperation Forums with African and Arab States.[31]

Over the last decade, the US and China have worked on a number of agreements, including the Strategic and Economic Dialogue (2009), the US–China Consultation on People-to-People Exchange (2010) and the Strategic Security Dialogue (2011). The US Agency for International Development has a China programme designed to 'protect and promote U.S. national interests and values'.[32]

The Congressional Research Service notes that the USA conducts provocative military operations in China's waters, particularly in China's Exclusive Economic Zone. The USA refuses to ratify the UN Convention on the Law of the Sea and therefore ignores China's claims to the zone. Incidents have occurred on at least three occasions between 2001 and 2009, when Chinese ships responded to US naval territorial invasions.

According to the US Congressional Research Service, the Obama administration announced its 'Pivot' to Asia in late-2011 'to devote more effort to influencing the development of the Asia–Pacific's norms', meaning to force China and other regional countries to follow US demands. It also involves 'deepen[ing] U.S. credibility in the region', meaning America's ability to intimidate and assert its dominance. The Asia Pivot includes a 'sustainable troop presence in the region' to bolster the so-called TPP 'free trade' deal, which the US set up for others to follow before withdrawing from it. The report also notes that as US (meaning US big business) 'economic interests' are 'shifting towards Asia' priorities are 'adjusted accordingly'. National Security Advisor Tom Donilon explained that the Pivot means ensuring that 'commerce and freedom of navigation are not impeded'.[33]

The same authors acknowledge that America's Asia Pivot is extremely dangerous and provocative, writing that it 'could strengthen the hand of Chinese hardliners' and 'potentially make it more difficult ... to gain China's cooperation on a range of issues', which naturally implies North Korea.[34]

Since the year 2000, says the CRS, Asia has been the USA's largest import market (mainly of US-owned products like iPhones which are assembled and re-imported to US domestic markets) and its second largest export market. Today, the Asia Pacific is of vital strategic significance to the USA, whose business and war planners seek to control and influence as much trade and commerce as possible. The Asia Pivot exists in large part due to 'the strategic importance of the energy resources and trade that pass through the Indian Ocean and the Straits of Malacca before reaching the manufacturing centers of East Asia'. The CRS report goes on to note that 50% of global container ships and 70% of oil and petroleum vessels transit the region.[35]

A later CRS report notes that 'China has extensive, though imprecise, claims to large parts of the SCS [South China Sea] ... [which] is bordered by a U.S. treaty ally, the Philippines, and is a key strategic waterway for the U.S. Navy'.[36]

The CRS report argues that a US 'failure' to 'emphasize' the importance of the Asia–Pacific 'could invite other regional powers, particularly China, to shape the region in ways that are not necessarily in U.S. interests'. What the people of the region want (Chinese influence, US influence or something entirely different, such as autonomy) is of zero interest and concern to the USA's war planners and policymaking elite.

'After the United States, Vietnam, and other East Asian countries diplomatically pushed back in 2010 against what they saw as Chinese encroachment in the South China Sea, China chose to join multilateral negotiations with Southeast Asian countries over a Code of Conduct in the South China Sea'. It is interesting to note that the US objects to China exerting influence in its own sea and region. Then-US Defense Secretary Leon Panetta said: 'reductions in U.S. defense spending will not – I repeat, will not – come at the expense of the Asia Pacific'.[37]

Two authors for the Council on Foreign Relations quote Edward Meade Earle, who said that grand strategy involves protecting 'vital interests ... against enemies, actual, potential, or merely presumed'. In other words, powerful actors like the USA can afford, in one sense, to imagine that they have enemies everywhere and try to convince their domestic populations (which do not usually support war) that hegemony is necessary for 'security'.[38]

The CFR authors advocate making the world a more dangerous, perhaps terminal, place by suggesting to US policymakers that a grand strategy be applied to countering, not cooperating with, China. They write that 'preserving U.S. primacy in the global system ought to remain the central objective of U.S. grand strategy in the twenty-first century'.[39]

China–North Korea relations: 'Emphasizing economic development'

Doug Bandow of the right-wing Cato Institute writes: 'China supports North Korea for several very practical reasons', mainly that NK 'impedes U.S. policy in East Asia. North Korea complicates American military planning, threatening Washington's leading military allies, South Korea and Japan, and causing them to divert resources that otherwise might be directed at China'.[40]

According to a report by an institute funded by the US government and led by numerous ex-government advisers, China's policy toward North Korea is 'to achieve stability by emphasizing economic development in North Korea'. This runs counter to US interests because, when it comes to North Korea (NK), China is pursuing its own interests within limits set by the USA and the US-led United Nations Security Council, as the report also concedes: 'These developments . . . demand an even more hard-nosed recognition of Chinese interests'.[41]

Unlike America's obstruction of diplomatic relations with NK, China, the report continues, has taken the opposite approach and been credited by the world outside the USA and its allies for having done so: 'China's North Korea policy in the early 2000s was seen by most observers as playing a constructive role in helping facilitate the Six-Party Talks and broker a diplomatic solution to resolve the political and security stand-off between North Korea and its neighbors'. These efforts have been frustrated by NK's insistence of continuing to pursue its nuclear deterrence, at least from China's perspective.[42]

NK is seen as something of a liability: China gets blamed by the USA for not restraining NK's actions and, with nuclear weapons supposedly in its possession, NK has some leverage against a dominant China. Ideally, China's ruling elite would presumably like to see the denuclearization of NK and the further opening of its economy to Chinese interests. The report also notes that China's main goals are 'avoiding conflict and ensuring a peaceful resolution of security issues on the Korean peninsula, promoting a stable political situation in North Korea, improving political and military relations with North Korea, and deflecting the influence of the other key players, particularly the United States and a strengthened U.S.-South Korea military alliance, in shaping outcomes on the peninsula that are contrary to Chinese interests'.[43]

Buying up North Korea
NK is largely dependent on China for oil and aid. The Chinese government is reluctant to disclose the amount of aid it gives to NK.

Despite Western claims that NK is a closed society, NK exports labour to 40 countries, including European, Asian and African ones. Kim Jong-un studied in Switzerland; added to which, Switzerland's Agape International began construction of an energy efficiency programme in NK. Singapore's Chosen Exchange is providing business programmes to the slowly reforming economy. Germany's Hanns Seidel Foundation is giving advice on reforestation.[44]

Chinese employers hire large numbers of North Koreans. The various UN Security Council Resolutions imposed on NK do not materially limit labour supply, so under stress from sanctions it is expected that NK-Chinese labour relations will expand. As NK's agricultural sector expands and mechanizes, Chinese experts are giving advice to NK on agricultural practices, healthcare and economic management.[45]

By the 1990s, China's diplomatic and financial interests centred more around South Korea than they did the North. This is a reflection of both China's and South Korea's then-newfound enthusiasm for US-led 'free market' economics (within limits, of course).[46]

America's Woodrow Wilson Center, whose board of directors includes numerous government employees, says that by 2003 China was NK's 'only remaining ally in the region'.[47]

Between 2002 and 2008, Chinese investment in NK increased from $1.5m to $42m, or 94% of NK's inward foreign direct investment. Between 2000 and 2009, NK's trade with China increased sixfold. In 2009, China and NK ended their nearly-20-year diplomatic hiatus when Chinese Premier Wen Jiabao visited in October to sign agreements on computer software, economic assistance, education programmes, tourism and wildlife 'protection'. Part of this integration has included the development of so-called green channels, with China being a leader in green technologies. NK companies have allegedly opened accounts in China, allowing them to convert the currency into US dollars, Euros, Yen and others.[48]

Despite fears among North Koreans that the country may became over-reliant on China, infrastructure and economic projects have continued. By January 2011, the Chinese had developed a route from Rason to shorten its own trading routes. NK leased its Rajin port to the Chinese for 40 years in 2015. In 2014, work began on the construction of the Juan river-Wonjong Bridge Highway between Hunchun and Rason. The aim is to increase traffic flows. In that year, work finished on the Yalu Bridge, a project funded by China to the tune of $292m, or 2bn Chinese Yuan. In September 2015, a high-speed train from Shenyang to Dandong on the border of NK began transporting Chinese tourists. China's Liaoning province is seeking to expand cross-border tourism with NK. Governors of the province are discussing the formation of economic zones. A few months later in December, NK announced new tourism rules concerning travel through the Economic Development Zones. NK hopes to host 2 million Chinese tourists by the year 2020.[49]

Despite US pressure, that China needs to 'resolve' the NK 'problem', China has ruled out launching attacks on NK facilities in the wake of further NK missile tests. Publicly, China advocates NK's denuclearization. Prior to its nuclear tests in 2013, China's NK policy was 'no war, no instability and no nuclear weapons'. This has changed to 'denuclearization, peace and stability and an early resumption of the Six-Party Talks', whose members are China, Japan, North Korea, Russia, South Korea and the USA. Relations were stretched in February 2013, when NK allegedly tested a third nuclear bomb. Chinese officials met with NK delegates less frequently and in 2014 NK seized and fined Chinese fishing boats allegedly in or near NK waters.[50]

In 2015, Liu Yunshan of the Chinese Standing Committee visited NK to celebrate 70 years of the so-called Workers' Party of Korea. There, he expressed hopes for denuclearization and advocated NK's pursuit of the Six-Party Talks. NK reciprocated by sending the Mudanbong band to play at Beijing's National Centre for the Performing Arts. The event was cancelled for reasons that remain unclear, leading many to suspect that NK seeks to deepen its relations with Russia.[51]

In 2016, after a series of alleged nuclear weapons tests, China agreed to UNSCR 2321, which restricted its coal exports to NK.[52]

Shen Dingli, of the Institute of International Studies in Shanghai, adds another dimension to the geopolitical analysis, namely the 'intrinsic[...]' connection between China, Taiwan and NK. China still considers the island of Taiwan to be part of China. America's behaviour towards Taiwan includes arming the country and conducting military exercises – all in provocation against China. NK 'acts as a guard post for China, keeping at bay the tens of thousands of U.S.

troops stationed in South Korea', hence the reduction of Chinese military deployment in northeast China and a closer focus on Taiwan.[53]

Shen writes:

> China merely provides [NK] with the means to survive, while [NK] acts as a bulwark against U.S. forces ... [I]f North Korea comes under a pre-emptive strike by the United States as a result of having developed nuclear weapons, China would then be obligated to assist its partner, as interpreted by the terms of that bilateral Treaty, if it is still effective ... In the face of North Korea's nuclear test, Japan and South Korea have two options: develop their own nuclear weapons or strengthen their alliances with the United States without developing their own nuclear weapons. They are more likely to choose the latter option, relying to a greater degree on the U.S. nuclear umbrella and missile defense system rather than developing their own nuclear weapons, a move that would provoke the United States itself and many other countries.[54]

What about China's current role in NK's missile programme? A series of CIA reports (2006–2010) on NK's nuclear capabilities do not identify China as the supplier of materials. Its 2007 report does, however, note that private Chinese businesses sell NK materials suitable for use in ballistic missile and nuclear programmes.[55]

The US–China–NK axis: 'China's greatest concern is reserved for the US military presence'

American military planners and business elites have a big problem: they are using China's substantial resources (particularly its population of 1.4bn relatively poor people) as a

source of exploitation (principally for electronics manufacturing). The sheer number of US products assembled in
China and the sheer volume of Chinese labourers has added
to the Chinese Gross Domestic Product boom, making it the
second largest economy in the world. But as economist Sean
Starrs and others have documented in extensive detail, most
of the profits from Chinese manufacturing in the hi-tech
sector go to US corporations.[56]

So China's 'boom' is a false economy in that its currency
remains weak (the exchange rate between it and the US dollar
is substantial), neoliberal reforms are leading to financiali-
zation (i.e., the Renminbi is being floated on international
markets) and profits are dependent on foreign investments
(mainly America's). China's huge GDP has allowed China to
increase its military spending consistently for 20 years. US
war planners and business elites are afraid that this level of
spending will allow China to pursue its own interests
(meaning the interests of China's political and business
elites) at the expense of US corporations.[57]

America's aim, then, is to encircle China with military
forces in order to 'contain' it and make sure China's markets
remain open to US businesses. China's efforts to counter this
are called Area Denial and Anti-Access in US military parlance. The US Congressional Research Service explains:
'"Area Denial/Anti-Access" strategies are those in which
adversaries attempt to erode the U.S. ability to project power
into what are, from the U.S. perspective, distant regions, and
from their standpoints, bordering areas'. If China has no right
to a particular area in Asia, what right does the US have,
besides the *de facto* right that the US is powerful enough to do
as its military planners wish? The US must therefore balance
seeing China as an ally open to US corporations and using

cheap Chinese labour, with portraying China as a threat: a regional power and potentially independent actor.[58]

North Korea sits in the middle of this matrix. The US has no significant investments in NK, so it is not dependent on the regime's survival the way it is dependent on keeping China as a simultaneous ally and enemy. The existence of a hostile, isolated NK enables the US to maintain its huge military presence in Japan and South Korea under the pretext of protecting South Korea and the region in general from NK. In reality, the US military presence is mostly aimed at China, with NK providing America with an excuse to maintain its military presence in the region. Without the 'threat' of NK, the US would have a hard time justifying such a massive military build-up around China, i.e. one of its key economic partners in the region.

As Chinese investment has poured into NK, particularly in the mining sector, US-led sanctions on NK minerals have harmed China's investments. China acquiesced in sanctioning NK because it too doesn't want NK to develop its alleged nuclear weapons. As a nuclear power, NK threatens China's prestige. However, China's 'greatest concern is reserved for U.S. military presence and robust U.S. alliance partnerships in Northeast Asia', writes Andrew Scobell, a political scientist at the military-linked RAND Corporation, who testified to the US–China Economic and Security Review Commission. 'From Beijing's point of view, Pyongyang's nuclear and missile programs are most problematic in that they trigger what China sees as threatening military responses by the United States and its allies'.[59]

Doug Bandow of the Cato Institute says that 'the Obama administration's approach has generally been to lecture [China], insisting that it follow American priorities. Unsurprisingly, successive Chinese leaders have balked'. Bandow notes that in the middle of this is North Korea, where 'an imploding, unstable, opaque, and brutal dictatorship with nuclear weapons might end up being the worst of all possible worlds'.[60]

2

The US and North Korea

Genocidal rhetoric: North Korea's 'extinction'

In August 2017, US President Donald Trump gave a speech to the press about America's 'opioid crisis' at the Trump National Golf Club. Trump was asked to comment on the political situation with North Korea.[61] He said,

> North Korea best not make any more threats to the United States. They will be met with fire and fury like the world has never seen. He [Kim Jong-un] has been very threatening beyond a normal state. And as I said, they will be met with fire, fury, and, frankly, power, the likes of which this world has never seen before.[62]

We shall examine North Korea's so-called threats to the USA throughout this book. Trump's words were surely designed (probably by speechwriters and advisers) to touch a nerve in North Korea. Few Westerners realize that during the Korean War, the USA destroyed 90% of the country (more than it did in Japan) with unprecedented carpet bombing (as we shall see).

Is Trump's violent persona unique, as the mainstream media infer? In 1993, the so-called liberal Bill Clinton stated that if North Korea ever used nuclear weapons, '[i]t would mean the end of their country as they know it'. So much for Trump taking an unusually hard line. Trump's 'fire and fury' echoes a Clinton-era plan to attack Iraq, eventually used by the military under the command of President George W. Bush, namely Shock and Awe. In 1996, the US National Defense University proposed inflicting an air war on a civilian population:[63]

> The intent here is to impose a regime of Shock and Awe through delivery of instant, nearly incomprehensible levels of massive destruction directed at influencing society writ large, meaning its leadership and public, rather than targeting directly against military or strategic objectives even with relatively few numbers or systems.[64]

This tactic was unleashed on Iraq in 2003 under the so-called neoconservative, Bush. Shock and Awe claimed 98,000 Iraqi lives in the first few months. The effects of the occupation went on to claim a million Iraqi lives.[65]

Although he supported the invasion of Iraq, Arizona Senator John McCain later spoke out against the aggressive persona of the Bush administration. McCain doubtless enacted this critical persona because his campaign managers sensed that the mood of the country was becoming more progressive, hence the election of Barack Obama in 2008 (who, unsurprisingly, turned out to be not so progressive). McCain famously ran against Obama. During the Bush years (2001–2009), McCain was dubbed a 'moderate' in the US corporate media. Given the politics of the period, 'moderate' meant right-winger. It was only after candidate Donald Trump was revealed to have admitted sexual assault ('I'm automatically attracted to beautiful [women] – I just start kissing them') that Senator McCain denounced the far-right Republican candidate in the 2016 election.[66]

On foreign policy, however, the once 'moderate' McCain wanted to out-do Trump and threatened genocide against

North Korea, saying that the price it would pay for 'aggression' would be 'extinction'. The most remarkable thing about McCain's threat was that no one, save progressive groups at the margins, responded.[67]

Korea: historical background: 'Anti-colonial struggle'

For centuries, Korea was a single entity. That ended in 1948.

The oldest known area which developed into modern Korea is Old Choson, now northwestern Korea and southern Manchuria. Old Choson was conquered by China in 108 BCE. Other kingdoms included Kaya (dominated by Japan and known as Mimana), Koguryŏ, Paekche and Silla. The dynasties fought for power and alliances frequently shifted. With help from China's Tang dynasty, Silla unified Korea, defeating Koguryŏ, Paekche and the Japanese protectorate, Kaya.[68]

Between 890 and 935 AD, some of the old dynasties had returned. Wang Kon founded Koryŏ (derived from Koguryŏ), expanding to the Yalu River and bringing the territory into conflict with Manchuria's Khitan dynasty. Wang agreed a peace treaty with Khitan, which placed much of the territory into Manchurian hands, thus severing links with China's Sung dynasty. By the early 1100s, however, the military had taken over and relations with Manchuria's Chin dynasty strained. The Mongols invaded in 1231. It took a century to drive them out.[69]

By far the most successful Korean dynasty was Choson (Yi), which lasted from 1392 in the aftermath of the Mongol defeat until 1910, when Western powers tried to take over the region. The Yi dynasty adopted Confucianism and fostered a distinctive culture (e.g., creating its own alphabet), fighting off Japanese invaders (who sought to use Korea as a route to conquer China) and Manchurian attacks. When the Manchus conquered China in 1644, however, Korea found itself politically isolated.[70]

By the late-18th century, Christianity introduced by Chinese and French Catholic missionaries was undermining Confucianism and Buddhism. In the 1860s–70s, Taewongun outlawed Christianity and repelled both French and US imperial invasions. In 1876, the Japanese forced Korea into a diplomatic agreement. In opposition to Japan, China facilitated Korean relations with the West, specifically the Korea–US treaty 1882. Having won victories over China and Russia, an empowered Japan annexed Choson in 1910.[71]

There is an ongoing dispute over islets (Tokdo/Takeshima).[72]

Having signed a Protectorate Treaty in 1905, Korea was gradually 'Japanized': its military, police, currency, financial policies and diplomatic relations dominated by the new regional empire. Japan formally annexed Korea between 1910 and 1919 in an effort to defeat the nationalist King Kojong and his guerrilla supporters. Millions of Korean civilians demonstrated peacefully against Japan's domination in the March First Movement, which was brutally suppressed. Japan responded by outlawing the Korean language and banning Korean names.[73]

The annual US Defense Department threat assessment to Congress (2012) says of North Korea: '[NK's] threat perceptions are shaped by a legacy of guerrilla warfare dating back to its anti-colonial struggle against the Japanese, political and economic isolation, experience during wartime, and a political culture that is defined by an unending existential struggle with outside forces'.[74]

The so-called communists of Korea and China have a long history, dating back to at least the 1930s, when Kim Il-sung waged his anti-Japanese fascist guerrilla war from Manchuria. The US government's US–China Economic and Security Commission notes that '[c]ontemporary diplomatic relations between China and North Korea (the Democratic People's Republic of Korea, or DPRK) are founded on the shared experience of fighting against Japan starting in the 1930s, Communist Party ties dating back to the 1920s, [and] shared wartime camaraderie from fighting together during the Korean War'.[75]

Pak Il-yu (later NK's Vice Prime Minister) also joined China's war against Japan. During China's civil war between 'communist' Mao and 'nationalist' (i.e., pro-US) Chiang Kai-shek, NK served as a significant base for Mao's forces, with 100,000 ethnic Koreans joining to fight for the Chinese 'communists'. Mao's Chinese People's Liberation Army consisted substantially of ethnic Koreans. During World War II, Kim Il-sung led anti-Japanese guerrilla forces in Manchuria.[76]

North–South: partition and war: 'We burned down every town in North Korea'

Korea faced the same fate as other victims of colonialism, including India–Pakistan and Israel–Palestine, namely it was partitioned by the so-called Great Powers of the time; in this case, the USSR and USA, working through the United Nations. Korea became the Democratic People's Republic of Korea (North Korea) and the Republic of Korea (South Korea).

The USSR and the USA, bitter enemies, both wanted the regimes in the two Koreas to be friendly to their interests. Both countries sought anti-Japanese puppets. Having a border with Russia made it easy for the USSR to support the so-called communist, Kim Il-sung. Russia supressed nationalist movements in the North and sponsored its puppet regime. In the South, the US helped crush the left and supported the Syngman Rhee regime. Both the US and the USSR refused to unify the countries, despite growing demands from ordinary Koreans.[77]

America's ongoing occupation of South Korea is a violation of the Cairo Declaration 1943, which states that Korea (then unified) shall be free and independent. Korea specialist Bruce Cumings leaves open the question whether NK invaded the South *in vacuo* or whether NK's actions were a response to South Korean provocation. Soviet archives opened in the wake of the USSR's collapse suggest that 'from February 1945 to April 1950 Stalin did *not* aim to gain control over the entire peninsula' (emphasis in original).[78]

The archives suggest that Stalin preferred a balance of power between North and South. Kathryn Weathersby of the Woodrow Wilson Center writes that Stalin was responding to Truman's plans 'to secure sole control over the occupation of Japan ... and to maintain China as a unified state under a government dependent on the United States'. In Eastern Europe, however, Stalin had more ambitious plans.[79]

In 1945, Soviet planners wrote that 'a Korea under Japanese rule would be a constant threat to the Far East of the USSR'. In August, Stalin approved the US plan to divide Korea between North and South and ordered Soviet forces to halt their advance. The border closures caused major disruptions to both sides. The Soviets proposed that Korea be placed under the joint trusteeship of the USA, UK, China and USSR as a step towards independence. In February 1947, after the US crushed the uprisings in the South, the North asked the Soviets to help in the unification of the country.[80]

In 1949, Kim Il-sung convinced Mao to allow over 50,000 Korean soldiers to leave the People's Liberation Army of China and join the Korean armed forces. Relations were strained when Kim failed to provide Mao with the details concerning Kim's imminent, planned invasion of the South.[81]

Mao and Chiang

Meanwhile, the anti-US leader of China, Chairman Mao, who had defeated the pro-US Chiang Kai-shek (who was based on the island territory Taiwan), wanted to invade Taiwan and make it formally part of China. The Soviets expected a war between North Korea and South Korea (which had no relation to the Taiwan issue) to occur later than it did. In June 1950, North Korea, apparently without consent from the USSR but using its weapons, illegally invaded the South. The USSR abstained from the UN Security Council, paving the way for the US-led resolutions 84 and 85 (1950) sanctioning North Korea. The resolution permits the formation of a unified military command to keep the peace. The resolution authorizes 'the unified command at its discretion to use the United Nations flag in the course of operations against North Korean force concurrently with the flags of the various nations participating'.[82]

In 1950, Stalin authorized Kim to unify North and South via military means. This was not, however, an order. Stalin never sent forces to support NK. Rather, Soviet forces invaded to support the Chinese forces in the country as part of the Soviet–Chinese defence agreement. US President Truman erroneously considered NK's attack on the South as a Soviet proxy manoeuvre 'to test Western resolve'. America's strategic position was one of retaining regional hegemony, namely 'defend[ing] Taiwan and the French position in Indochina'.

Other aims were 'to solidify NATO, and to rearm West Germany'.[83]

Those who gave birth to America's extreme right-wing neocon movement in the 1990s, found their way into the post-War State Department, particularly Paul Nitze who replaced George Kennan as chief of Policy Planning. Nitze, reflecting the paranoia of Pentagon planners, was convinced that the Soviets sought 'to impose ... absolute authority over the rest of the world'.[84]

China supplied 1.3 million troops to fight the Americans in the Korean War. In 1950, opposing factions in the Korean Workers' Party attempted a coup against Kim. It failed due to Mao's support. In July 1951, after the armistice talks, China strove to control NK's railway system, but Kim resisted, straining China–NK ties further. In 1953, China pressured Kim to resist an armistice.[85]

Fire and Fury

The UN Forces operating in Korea were in reality primarily US forces. They were led by General Douglas McArthur and included combat units from US allies: the UK, Australia, South Africa, Turkey and others. Very quickly, Kim Il-sung's forces were defeated and pushed across the dividing line, the 38th parallel. The US then escalated the war by invading North Korea. Chairman Mao of China warned the US that China would enter the war if US forces approached the Yalu River, which borders China. By October, US forces had captured North Korea's capital, Pyongyang. Chinese fighters were quickly defeated. Within a month, however, the Chinese forces had regrouped and, with McArthur's forces overstretched, Kim's forces recaptured Pyongyang in December.[86]

By January 1951, Kim captured Seoul, South Korea. Fierce

fighting (Operation Killer) repelled Chinese forces from the South and the US recaptured Seoul in March and had again pushed beyond the 38th parallel by April. The US manufactured F-86 Sabres in an effort to counter Russian-made Chinese MiGs. The US ruthlessly targeted civilian infrastructure, including dams, rice paddies, bridges, trains and industrial centres. About two million North Koreans were slaughtered, compared to 1.3 million South Koreans.[87]

In June, the UN brokered talks with the USSR, which dragged out for two years. One sticking issue was that Northern Korean forces were so brutalized by their own command, many didn't want to return and fight. The peace talks included a proposal that prisoners of war be returned of their own free will to their respective armies; a proposal which the North Korean leadership rejected.[88]

General Curtis LeMay, head of the US Strategic Air Command, later said that because the Pentagon refused to authorize carpet bombing in certain areas, the war dragged out. Either way, LeMay boasts of murdering hundreds of thousands of people. '[W]e went over there and fought the war and eventually burned down every town in North Korea ... Over a period of three years or so, we killed off ... twenty percent of the population of Korea as direct casualties of war, or from starvation and exposure'. By May 1953, US air strategy turned to destroying North Korea's food supply by flooding rice fields with targeted attacks on dams. The US set 'to work burning five major cities in North Korea to the ground, and ... destroy[ing] completely every one of about 18 major targets', in the words of Major General Emmett O'Donnell of the Strategic Air Command.[89]

Dean Rusk, who served in Truman's State Department, explained: 'We were bombing with conventional weapons' —

i.e., non-nuclear — 'everything that moved in North Korea, every brick standing on top of another'. Historian Charles K. Armstrong cites US Air Force estimates, that the destruction in North Korea alone, a country the size of Pennsylvania, was greater than the damage wrought on Japan, 70% of which was destroyed by the USA. Having dropped 635,000 tonnes of explosives on North Korea, including napalm, the US ran out of targets.[90]

In 1952, during the so-called ceasefire, Truman discussed the possibility in a secret memo of 'all-out war. It means that Moscow, St. Petersburg, Mukden, Vladivostok, Peking, Shanghai, Port Arthur, Darien, Odessa, Stalingrad and every manufacturing plant in China and the Soviet Union will be eliminated', referring to what would have been the third-plus US use of nuclear weapons after Hiroshima and Nagasaki.[91]

North Korea: the Cold War and after: 'Stiffening quills, retreating into its shell'

Kim Il-sung immediately consolidated power, purging the Korean People's Army of Pak Il-Yu and Mu Chong of the Yan'an faction of the Korean Workers' Party. Because Mao had promised Kim that China would prop up the country without too much interference in its political system, Kim avoided purging any Chinese 'communists' during his coup.[92]

In 1956 at the KWP Central Committee Plenary Session, the Yan'an and pro-Soviet factions of the KWP denounced Kim's cult of personality. This only led to him expelling four top officials to China and forcing others to seek asylum in the USSR.[93]

In 1958, following a disagreement with Mao over Kim's purges and a refusal on the part of Mao to turn over the defectors, Mao withdrew all Chinese troops from NK.[94]

After the US decimated North Korea in the early-1950s, the Soviet countries and their allies facilitated the NK's reconstruction.[95]

In 1959, the USSR built the Yongbyon Nuclear Scientific Research Centre in NK with the aim of helping the country develop nuclear energy. The USSR stopped short of providing uranium and plutonium.[96]

'Through the 1950s and 1960s, following the end of the Korean War, Japan made no response to overtures from North Korea for normalization other than to encourage as many Japan-resident Koreans as possible to repatriate themselves to North Korea', writes historian Gavan McCormack.[97]

In 1961, China and NK signed the Treaty of Friendship, Co-operation and Mutual Assistance, obliging signatories to take measures preventing aggression by any state. Given China's current, increasingly hard line against NK via US-led sanctions, NK questions China's commitment to the Treaty.[98]

NK–Soviet relations were strained after the death of Stalin and the birth of Khrushchev's de-Stalinization programmes. After the Soviet–China split, NK cemented its relations with China; until, that is, the dawn of China's Cultural Revolution. The so-called Cultural Revolution made Kim a target of criticism. The path toward reconciliation was laid in 1968, when NK captured the crew of a US intelligence vessel, *Pueblo*. During this period, China announced that NK represented the whole of Korea.[99]

In the 1980s, NK began construction of 5-megawatt uranium graphite nuclear reactors, capable of producing 6kg of weapons-grade plutonium per annum. In response, the US pressured the Soviets to encourage NK to accede to the Nuclear Non-Proliferation Treaty. The USSR failed to honour its obligations toward NK and NK never permitted inspections by the International Atomic Energy Agency, as required by the NPT.[100]

After the 1988 Olympics held in Seoul, South Korea, the USSR and China decided to strengthen their ties. Russia failed to renew its Soviet-era Agreement on Friendship, Cooperation and Mutual Assistance with NK. In 1992, China announced a new era of cooperation with NK's US-occupied neighbour, South Korea.[101]

NK took all of these events in bad faith, and according to Fu Ying, a former diplomat for China, encouraged NK to 'go it alone'. As the USA deepened ties with a newly de-Sovietized Russia, 'free market' China and 'free market' South Korea, it too ignored NK. The pattern emerging here is that NK hasn't so much chosen isolation; rather, it has been isolated.[102]

NK's relations with Soviet countries and allies ended in 1989. South Korea's state controlled, industrialized and prosperous economy began adopting US-style 'free market' reforms which continue to the present. South Korea absorbed NK's ex-Soviet allies into its trade and investment sphere (Nordpolitik).[103]

With the collapse of the Soviet Union, NK lost the protection of the Soviet nuclear umbrella. 'Sometimes portrayed as an aggressive, threatening state, the more appropriate images for North Korea may rather be those of a porcupine or snail: stiffening its quills or retreating into its shell in fear to attempt to resist contact with a hostile outside world', writes Gavan McCormack.[104]

NK has been accused of being a state-sponsor of terrorism. However, a US Congressional Research Service report published in late 2006 states: 'North Korea was added to the U.S. list of state-sponsors of terrorism in 1988 and remains on the list, although it is not known to have sponsored any terrorist acts since 1987.'[105]

In 1994, the US and EU established the Korean Peninsula Energy Development Organization under the Agreed Framework. This has involved EU monitors providing safety checks and expertise.[106]

In 1995, NK accepted humanitarian assistance from the EU and USA, with NGOs active in providing water sanitation and food security. By 2000, however, many, with the exception of EU NGOs, had ceased operating due to the regime's strict controls over their activities. In the same year, the British Embassy initiated an English language and teacher-training programme. Partly as a result of these and other measures, Pyongyang University of Science and Technology had openings for teaching positions, including for Korean-Americans.[107]

In 1998, the EU established a political dialogue under the European External Action Service. The European Union used South Korea–Russia's Nordpolitik as an opportunity to develop links with North Korea; specifically, most of the Central and Eastern European states joined the European Union between 2004 and 2007, totalling eight diplomatic missions inside NK. The EU's trade with NK is less than 1% of NK's total trade and investment, most of which comes in the form of aid and development.[108]

In 2000 (under Bill Clinton), NK and the USA signed a joint statement recognizing that 'international terrorism poses an unacceptable threat to global security and peace, and that terrorism should be opposed in all its forms'. In 2001, NK signed the Convention for the Suppression of Financing Terrorism.[109]

3

North Korea and the Rest of the World

North Korea–South Korea: 'The Vietnam war caused NK to act when it did'

A US military report states that after hostilities ended in 1953, both the Korean Armistice Agreement of that year and the Geneva Conference 1954 left open the possibility of further conflagration. The report says that both NK and South Korea issued threats to each other, with President Syngman Rhee (America's puppet in the South) threatening 'unification by marching northward'.[110]

Earlier in the book, we cited and quoted US Air Force estimates of the immense damage inflicted by the US on the North. The military report suggests that this level of destruction affected future prospects for peace: 'Due to war-time damage and the moderating influence of their powerful Chinese and American allies, neither the north nor the south attempted to take serious steps toward implementing their reunification schemes'.[111]

In 1956, the US floated the idea of installing nuclear weapons in South Korea. Having destroyed 90% of North Korea with conventional weapons and having publicly touted the idea of nuking the North, the proposal to station weapons of mass destruction in the South was a major provocation.[112]

This violated the Korean Armistice Agreement, which states that neither side introduce new weapons systems. The US formally announced its intention to violate the Agreement and station nuclear and non-nuclear weapons in the South. One of NK's responses was to build deep, underground facilities.[113]

A report by the CIA acknowledges that in the immediate post-Korean War years, the North impressed South Koreans with its economic progress. This occurred at a time when the South was under the ruinous oppression of Syngman Rhee. The US feared that South Koreans might press for democratic reforms or work with the North to overthrow the US puppet. '[E]xcellent progress towards ... rapid industrialization and the achievement of a high degree of self-sufficiency ... aroused admiration among some South Koreans', says the CIA report.[114]

After the North's economy slowed (due in part to the shift of allegiance on the part of NK from the Soviets to the Chinese), the condition of the South improved. With the new dictator, Park, in power in the South, coupled with Japanese (meaning US) economic loans, the situation in the South improved for the USA. NK's 'inability ... to exploit unrest in the South ... has probably been a factor in its decision to adopt violent tactics'.[115]

Vietnam War Provokes N.K.

The CIA acknowledges that, following the end of WWII, there was 'more than a decade of relative quiet'. Beginning October 1966, NK apparently initiated hostilities. The CIA concludes: 'the war in Vietnam probably caused North Korea to act when it did'. The CIA tacitly acknowledges that NK (rightly or wrongly) considered its actions a genuine pre-emptive strategy to deter further US aggression in Asia, writing: '[NK] has ... been apprehensive that the conflict in Southeast Asia might spread to China and thence ultimately to Korea'. NK's fears were worsened by the then-weakened alliances with the

Soviets and Chinese. Because Moscow failed to intervene in Cuba and Vietnam, NK reasoned that the Soviets would not intervene to deter a US attack on the North.[116]

Perhaps even more important, the CIA reckons that NK launched its 'small' attacks on the South in response to the latter's participation in the Vietnam War. Such attacks 'put certain pressures on the [South Korean] government, particularly in connection with its participation in the Vietnamese War'.[117]

By 1967, the US had deployed 3,200 nuclear weapons to the Pacific, most of which were stationed in South Korea and Okinawa.[118]

Earlier, we found no evidence of a 'communist' conspiracy involving Soviets or Chinese. Likewise, the then-classified CIA report (1968) confirms that heightened NK activity along the border was not the result of a plot from either of the so-called communist powers. 'We believe that North Korea undertook its program of violence of its own volition, not under pressure from either Moscow or Peking, and that this program does not indicate a present Communist intention to invade South Korea'.[119]

The CIA report also acknowledged the low probability of all-out war, writing: 'there is probably no intention of escalating the demilitarized zone (DMZ) attacks to a point at which open warfare might result'. Later in the book, we shall examine America's modern threat assessments which continue to refute the mainstream media claim that NK poses a regional threat militarily. Even in the late-1960s, the CIA was secretly acknowledging that NK forces 'could not mount a sustained attack against the South without a large volume of material help from outside'.[120]

The report concludes that by the late-1960s, the NK 'navy' was 'essentially a coastal patrol and inshore defense force'. The Air Force, however, was supposedly 'superior to that of South Korea', but vastly inferior to the US Air Force. Likewise, a US military report states that, '[p]owerful as the North Korean forces appeared, when placed in the full context of the conventional balance on the peninsula, the Communists did not possess a militarily significant advantage in combat power'.[121]

After the adoption of the US–South Korean Presidential Instruction No. 18, which expanded low-level military operations, NK responded by invading South Korea in 1968 with a team of commandos, Unit 124, who sought to murder Park. Due to mistakes made by the commandos (which raises questions about the true objective of the mission), they were caught and some were killed. In the same year, the American spy ship, USS *Pueblo*, was on its way to gather intelligence on NK. The North Korean navy captured the vessel and tortured the American spies.[122]

With regard to the assassination attempt, now declassified cables from Soviet Romania state: 'Judging from the way the North Korean press is presenting the situation in the ROK [South Korea], we realize that they are exaggerating a great deal and they purposely distort the truth so as to create the impression of a truly revolutionary state of mind'. They add: 'the North Koreans are currently testing the nerves and feeling out the attitudes of all elements in South Korea, including the US, towards a potential large-scale military confrontation'.[123]

Concerning the USS *Pueblo* incident: 'this provocative act directed at gathering intelligence was the most outrageous one [committed by the United States] since signing the Armistice' (square brackets added by translators).[124]

These cables cannot be dismissed as 100% Soviet propaganda because a) NK's Soviet allies disapproved of NK's actions in both cases and, b) they did not offer military, diplomatic or ideological assistance to NK, preferring to remain 'neutral' on the matter, except in the *Pueblo* case where it was advised that the Soviets use it as an excuse to condemn the US at the United Nations.

Skirmishes

Emboldened by these actions, NK became more provocative and intolerant of US–SK border activities, such as cutting down trees and approaching NK guard posts.

In April 1969, North Korea shot down a US Navy spy plane (the EC-121). In December of that year, NK agents hijacked a South Korean airliner (the YS-11). The US escalated hostilities by shooting NK spies in the South and flying helicopters over the DMZ. In January, an NK agent hijacked a Korean Airlines flight. The plane crashed and the hijacker was killed.[125]

In July 1972, North and South entered into an historic agreement concerning the bilateral reunification of Korea. Both sides agreed that reunification had to be agreed 'internally' and 'without the use of military forces', that 'measures to stop military provocation' should be fostered and that 'an atmosphere of mutual trust' be cultivated.[126]

By October, South Korea had violated the terms of the agreement when Park imposed the hardline Yushin Constitution in the South and consolidated power, personally selecting the National Conference for Unification officials.[127]

At first, NK responded with rhetoric concerning unilateral reunification plans and futile efforts to diplomatically isolate the South from the rest of the world. NK then expanded its peace offers to include the USA. As Shin Jong-dae, a scholar at the Woodrow Wilson Center reports: 'the United States dared not respond positively to North Korea's overture in the mid-1970s'; or, one might add, at any time, for fear of looking weak.[128]

In August 1974, a Japanese-born North Korean sympathizer, Mun Se-gwang, made an assassination attempt on Park, but missed and murdered his wife, Yuk Young-soo.

Phases of U.S. Expansion

With Park's hardline policies in place, the North revitalized its military. Throughout the late-1960s and up to the early-1990s, NK captured crews and sank South Korean boats and vessels which it claimed had strayed too close to its waters.

The US and South Korea have conducted military exercises near North Korea since the end of the Korean War. North Korea has never conducted military exercises near the continental United States. A report by Robert Collins, former Pentagon and Korea serviceman, published by an institute of Johns Hopkins University, divides US–South Korea military exercises into four phases.

Phase 1: The first exercises took place between 1955 and 1957 (Autumn Season and Spring Shower). Others included Counterblow and Strong Shield. These incorporated counterinsurgency operations, for as we have seen NK had some ideological support in the South and conducted frequent infiltration operations. The decade ended with the establishment of the US Unified Command Plan, which included the replacement of the Far East Command with the Pacific Command. At this point, the United Nations Command for South Korea (meaning the US military) moved from Tokyo (Japan) to Seoul, South Korea.[129]

Phase 2: NK reacted to these developments and those outlined above by engaging in provocations against the South. NK's decision to relocate its armed forces to the DMZ (i.e., closer to South Korea) had the effect of 'reducing warning time and complicating battlefield defense strategies for the alliance'. The US–South Korean exercises, now called Focus Lens (aka Focus Retina) began in 1968 and included long-range US flights designed to demonstrate the rapidity of US force deployment.[130]

Phase 3: The '70s to the '90s were a time of increased NK provocations. However, scholars and media have ignored the fact that from 1976 to 1991 there was 'an increase in the size of combined ROK–US exercises'. These included the establishment of the ROK–US Combined Forces Command. Focus Lens became an integrated exercise involving the SK government. '[U]ltimately bec[oming] the largest computer-assisted simulation in the world', the war game was dubbed Ulchi Focus Lens.[131]

In addition to the above, the new exercise Team Spirit was introduced in 1976. By the late '80s, Team Spirit had grown from a force numbering 107,000 to over 200,000. Ex-Korean serviceman Robert Collins states: 'Because of its size, Team Spirit became a major concern for the North Koreans'.[132]

Interestingly, Collins infers that NK's efforts to build nuclear weapons and devise a strategy was in large measure a response to an expanded Team Spirit: 'North Korean capabilities began to go "asymmetric," namely by fielding of non-conventional weapons systems that were extremely difficult to counter with conventional forces'.[133]

Phase 4: The US began incorporating NK's potential nuclear strategy into Team Spirit. Designing war games to counter what was then a non-existent threat from nuclear weapons meant that the US and South Korea had to expand their own capabilities. This only served to escalate the situation. NK deployed long-range artillery near the DMZ with the aim of having the potential to strike Seoul.[134]

Collins describes Team Spirit as a 'carrot and a stick'. The 1992 exercise was cancelled until 1993 and not conducted again until 1996, 'as a result of negotiations that led to the 1994 [Agreed Framework]', which, as we shall see, the US violated. From 1994 to 2007, Team Spirit was replaced by Foal Eagle and the smaller-scale Reception, Staging, Onward Movement and Integration. Also in 2007, Ulchi Focus Lens was replaced by Ulchi Freedom Guardian.[135]

Since Collins published the report, the US has entered into a fifth phase of its military strategy towards NK. Writing in *National Interest*, Michael Peck reports on the classified Operations Plan 5015, parts of which have been reported in the Japanese and South Korean press. The foreign press claim that OPLAN 5015 involves contingencies for guerrilla conflict and assassination. An expanded Foal Eagle involves 4D: detect, disrupt, destroy and defend against NK's supposed nuclear arsenal. In other words, committing aggression against NK. Members of South Korea's parliament were furious over the government's refusal to disclose details of OPLAN 5015.[136]

Crab Wars

As is usually the case when outside imperial powers interfere in the internal affairs of countries and split them apart, the division of Korea left unresolved border disputes.

Hwanghae was one of the eight provinces of Korea during the Choson kingdom. The Northern Limit Line (NLL) is a disputed demarcation in the Yellow Sea. The NLL *de facto* ceded the Yeonpyeong and Baengnyeongdo islands to South Korea. The Armistice Agreement 1953 reaffirmed that the islands fall under South Korea's sovereignty but left open the maritime demarcation line.

A declassified CIA report states that in late-1973 and early-1974, NK began a series of 'minor' provocations, '[t]he purpose of [which includes bolstering NK's claim to] the waters surrounding each of the five island groups ... as part of its territorial sea'. It goes on to note that '[c]ontiguous waters ... are not defined' and that '[t]he NLL ... has no basis in international law, nor does it conform along some of its length to even minimal provisions regarding the division of territorial waters'.[137]

A US State Department cable from 1973 states: 'We are aware of no evidence that NLL has ever been officially presented to North Koreans' (all upper case in original). Crucially, it goes on to say that '[w]e would be in an extremely vulnerable position of charging them with penetrations beyond a line they have never accepted or acknowledged'. In addition to the objective facts, the cables give some insight into how propaganda works in the USA. The State Department officials then go on to suggest changes to the text for public relations, including: 'The words "Armistice Regime" should be deleted and the words "Peace and Stability of Korea" inserted'. And '[text] should be revised as follows: "The Northern Limit Line has played an important role in preserving peace in the waters for the past twenty years" '; this despite the fact that the cable acknowledges it as a source of friction.[138]

In 1999, NK began a series of operations ranging from interceptions to attacks around the disputed islands.

According to legal scholar Jon Van Dyke, the NLL divides

Korea's fishing waters 'and blocks North Korea's access to the fishing resources in … part of the Yellow (West) Sea'. Of particular concern is the issue of blue crabs, a delicacy traded regionally. China, for instance, 'illegally harvest[s] the blue crabs'.[139]

In June 1999, NK despatched navy patrol boats and fishing boats to the NLL. South Korea responded by conducting manoeuvres to prevent the NK forces from crossing the line. Over the coming days, NK damaged a SK navy fast boat and the South responded by bumping NK's boats. On June 14, NK raised a white flag between Socheongdo and Yeonpyeong. The next day, both sides engaged in bumping operations which ended in exchanges of gunfire. Crabs, says Van Dyke, were the trigger.[140]

Remarkably, NK issued the following statement in July: 'Feeling regretful for the unforeseen armed clash … [W]e are aware of the view that both sides should make joint efforts to prevent the recurrence of similar incidents in the future'. No further action was taken. In September 1999, NK unilaterally drew a maritime boundary. SK President Roh responded by promoting the idea of a joint fishery zone.[141]

A skirmish similar to the one described above occurred in June 2002, latter dubbed the Second Battle of Yeonpyeong.

SK's hardline President Lee rejected the joint fishery zone proposal mentioned above. For Lee, the NLL is '[a] critical border that contributes to keeping peace on our land'. This appears to have been plagiarized from the US State Department cables quoted above.[142]

In 2009, both sides fought the Battle of Daecheong. In November of that year, a NK patrol boat entered the NLL. SK fired warning shots and NK returned fire.[143]

In March 2010, South Korea's *Cheonan* warship sank. A

team of investigators from the USA, South Korea, Australia, Britain, Canada and Sweden pointed the finger at NK, while China, Russia and NK itself denied responsibility. The media largely neglected to mention that the sinking took place during US–SK military exercises. Initially, the SK Ministry of Defence denied any NK involvement. A SK investigator, Shin Sang-cheol, was ejected by the SK MoD from the National Assembly after he testified that he saw corpses bearing no signs of death from explosion and that, in writing to then-US Secretary of State Hillary Clinton, evidence had been tampered with.[144]

A year later, the Bombardment of Yeonpyeong occurred. NK requested that the South halt its military exercises. In response to SK's exercises, the North deployed MiGs to the region and fired shells, some of which landed on the island. The South escalated tensions by returning fire. Events continued and casualties mounted.

The Kaesong Industrial Complex

One of the few positive steps taken between NK and South Korea has been the development of the Kaesong Industrial Complex (KIC), an administrative region designed to strengthen economic ties between the two countries.

The Kaesong Industrial Complex was opened by South Korea in December 2004. The North and South developed taxation and accountancy codes. Pyongyang hired SK's Hyundai Asan to develop the area. The South sees the KIC as low-cost labour competition against China, which also uses cheap NK labour. Parts assembled and produced in the KIC include textiles, machine parts and chemical products. The number of NK workers in the KIC is estimated to be in excess of 47,000.[145]

None of the DMZ and island conflicts outlined above were deemed serious enough by either side to close the KIC. However, in 2007 President Lee cancelled a number of infrastructure projects, including the building of dormitories for NK workers. The South Korean Ministry of Unification estimates that 99.6% of the two country's bilateral trade and investment occur via the KIC. After NK's fourth nuclear weapons test in January 2016, South Korea closed the KIC. One of the effects has been to strengthen NK–Chinese economic ties.[146]

NK–Japanese relations: 'North Korea cannot survive without food and oil'

Having been under its occupation from 1910 to 1945 and then having seen the country become a puppet of the USA, Koreans, particularly North Koreans, are wary of Japan. The NK regime has treated Japanese people despicably. By 1982, NK had kidnapped 13 Japanese civilians, including a 13-year-old girl, as well as couples and students, for no apparent reason other than perhaps turning them into spies. At least eight of the 13 died.[147]

And yet by 1990, Japan's three main political parties issued a declaration of intent to normalize relations with NK. Negotiations lasted for two years. US pressure ended the negotiations. NK continued testing missiles and spying on Japanese waters, refusing to publicly thank Japan for rice aid during the notorious '90s famine.[148]

The *New York Times* reports that in 1998, after NK fired a missile over Japan (which it claimed was part of a satellite launch), NK adopted a moratorium on long-range missile tests. SK's Kim Dae-jong initiated a 'sunshine' policy toward NK, culminating in the summit of June 2000. With Japan resuming normalization talks in April and rumours of secret US negotiations in October, things looked brighter. But George W. Bush stole the US election in 2000 and ushered in a new era of hardline policies.[149]

In 1995, Japan's Prime Minister Murayama Tomiichi issued an apology for the pain caused by the empire. This led to the signing of the Japan–South Korea Joint Declaration in 1998. In 2005, however, SK's hardline President Roh Moo-hyun denounced Tomiichi's statement and Joint Declaration as inadequate.[150]

Gunfire was exchanged between NK and Japan in December 2001. This was the Battle of Amami-Ôshima, or Spy Ship incident. This involved an encounter in the East China Sea where the Japanese Defence Intelligence Head-quarters alleged that an NK spy vessel was operating in Japan's exclusive economic zone. The Japanese Coast Guard was sent out and ended up killing, directly or indirectly, 15 North Koreans.[151]

In September 2002, Japanese PM Koizumi met with Kim Jong-il to apologize for Japan's colonial crimes and offer NK loans, credits and aid grants via the Japan Bank for International Co-operation. Part of the agreement was that both sides would waive all property claims stemming from Japan's imperial past. A security and mutual assurance guarantee was also included. In return, Kim apologized for abducting Japanese civilians between 1977 and 1982 and for the incursions into Japanese territory.

By October 2002, Japan reneged on its agreements, failing to return Japanese civilians to NK who had been abducted in the '70s and '80s and who had sought brief repatriation in Japan. Later, PM Shinzo Abe (then Deputy Chief of the Cabinet) made provocative and threatening statements, that NK 'cannot survive without ... food and oil'.[152]

Historian McCormack writes:

> North Korea was left with few options. With its pleas for lifting of the financial sanctions and/or for direct talks with the U.S. ignored, its discussions with Japan on the abductions at a dead end, trade being slowly stifled and military intimidation stepped up, it responded in July with the launch of seven Scud, Nodong and Taepodong missiles into seas adjacent to the Russian Far East, followed three months later with its first nuclear test.[153]

Japan launched spy satellites over NK in 2003, violating the moratorium on long-range testing.[154]

After 2006, with the hardliner Abe now in power in Japan, the media launched an anti-NK propaganda offensive. Japanese Koreans suffered as a result. By 2008 there were 610,000 Korean residents in Japan, of whom 25% are affiliated with NK. Abe's government stripped many of their lands by auctioning it and revoking their preferential tax status. Far-righters in Japan launched arson attacks on the country's Korean community. One elderly Japanese Korean, heavily dependent on intravenous drugs, had her home and associates' homes raided by 100 Japanese police investigators who claimed she was part of a NK biological weapons and materials smuggling programme.[155]

Returning to geopolitics, Abe's successor PM Asō balked at very brief US efforts to normalize relations with NK, while the cabinet considered it a betrayal. South Korea signed the General Security of Military Information Agreement (GSOMIA) with Japan in November 2016. Around the same time, South Korea increased its military budget.[156]

Of strategic significance to NK is the East China Sea, where Japan has ongoing territorial disputes with China. The main bone of contention is with islets including the Senkakus and Diaoyu Dao. These islets are protected *de facto* by the USA under the Treaty of Mutual Cooperation and Security with Japan.[157]

Russia–North Korea: 'Economic relations expanded alarmingly'

Like China and the USA, Russia has regional ambitions in the Asia Pacific, not least because part of its vast territory lies there. Unlike the USA, however, Russia and China are not powerful enough to have significant military influence in the region. Given the sizes of their relative economies, they are potentially big economic players.

The RAND Corporation suggests that during the Cold War, NK's strategic interests were more with China than the USSR, the relations with whom are described as 'cool'. The Soviets were 'unsympathetic' to Kim Il-sung's supposed policy of self-reliance.[158]

As we saw earlier, Russia and NK were military allies until 1991, when the newly-de-Sovietized Russia revoked its agreement with NK and began negotiating with South Korea.[159]

In 2003, for the first time Russia entered into international negotiations over NK's nuclear weapons programme, which Russia opposes. Russia is also a member of the Six Party Talks.[160]

Between 2006 and 2008, Russia, NK and South Korea discussed construction of a Trans-Siberian Railroad extension, known as the Trans-Korean Railroad. But with Lee in power, the South rejected the plan. Russia and NK completed a phase of the project in 2011. The railway has been used to transport coal from Russia to China and South Korea.[161]

Russia's main export is energy. It is self-sufficient in gas and coal and seeks to run pipelines to South Korea via the North. In 2011, trilateral negotiations between the three countries began on the prospect of pipelines, namely the Intergovernmental Commission, which has held regular meetings with NK. Hecker and Carlin, in *The Bulletin of the Atomic Scientists*, write: 'Economic relations with Russia stirred again, while those with China expanded vigorously and, some might say, alarmingly'. 'Some' meaning the USA. This shows that America's leaders are more committed to keeping NK isolated, in the hope of collapsing the regime at the expense of regional and even global peace.[162]

In August 2011, Kim Jong-il met Russian President Dmitry Medvedev. Around the same time, there was a test of the east coast rail line from Rason (NK) to the Tumen River (shared with Russia). The three countries also discussed agriculture, construction, shipbuilding and timber processing.[163]

China uses energy as a bargaining chip over NK, much in the way that Russia does with Ukraine. As a result of inter-mittent and, since the sanctions, reduced oil flows from China, NK is relying more heavily on oil purchased from Russia (as opposed to provided in the form of humanitarian aid).[164]

In order to bolster the interests of Russia's economic elites, President Vladimir Putin developed a strategy towards Northeast Asia and the Korea Peninsula, creating in 2012 the Far East Development Ministry. Unlike China, Russia has significant energy reserves it hopes to sell regionally. Putin suggested that a nuclear-armed NK was a threat to Russia's interests. Unlike successive US policies, Putin suggested integrating NK into the regional economy. Part of Putin's plan included the cancelling of 90% of NK's $11bn debt, which many viewed as a move towards a debt-for-aid agenda. Unlike China, Russia does not desire using NK as a buffer between itself and South Korea and the USA because it sees NK as too unstable.[165]

NK's remaining debt would be held as credit by Vnesh-econombank, meaning that construction projects in NK would be owned *de facto* by Russia. By 2013, Russia was employing 35,000 North Koreans in construction, fishing and other labour-intensive industries. In September 2014, NK signed a so-called Victory contract with Russia with the aim of bringing extracted NK minerals to Russian markets. The deal was supposedly worth $25bn. Russia declared 2015 the Year of Friendship between Russia and NK, with a delegation from the latter participating in the Eastern Economic Forum in September.[166]

In May 2017, Russia and NK developed a ferry service between Vladivostok and Rajin.[167]

North Korea's economy: Moving towards 'free markets'?

NK's mineral wealth is estimated by many, including the South Korean government, to be worth a minimum of $3 trillion, hence the massive investment in NK infrastructure by China and US efforts to isolate the country economically.[168]

Since its founding in 1949, NK has pursued *Juche*, or economic self-reliance. This inherently makes NK an enemy of the USA, which seeks to open up markets for its businesses around the world. Over the last decade, NK has been making a slow transition from totalitarian state control ('socialism' in the propaganda parlance of the NK state) over markets, production and finance, toward profit-making for business and entrepreneurs ('free markets' in the propaganda parlance of Western politicians and economists). The Kim family has never admitted this, as it would betray their self-professed 'communist' principles. But the reality suggests that the seeds of reform have been planted.[169]

The difficulty for the USA is that if NK pursues open 'free markets' (as the US wants every country to do), those open markets might be led by Chinese investors and producers, thereby undermining US access. Already, Chinese businesses enjoy a 90% share of NK's foreign trade and investment (over 30% of which is in textiles). Perhaps ironically, America's constant threats against NK, and especially the economic sanctions imposed over the years, have slowed the very economic reforms that it appears to want to see take place. Like the USA, NK is a military economy: *Songun*. But unlike the USA, NK's military spending does not stimulate a hi-tech economy, or indeed much of any economy.[170]

Despite relentless Western media frames depicting NK as an entirely impoverished, backward state, the reality is that in the capital, Pyongyang, many now use cell phones, buy (mainly Chinese) products from malls and often get stuck in traffic. Of course, it's a different story in the rural areas, but it is a more dynamic economy and society than Western media propaganda would have us believe. NK's major problem is its reliance on imported oil, which is needed for its outdated agricultural machinery. According to the UN Food and Agricultural Organization, NK's lack of fuel self-sufficiency contributes to its inability to meet domestic food demands.[171]

Until 2009, NK imposed tight regulations on its economy. Kim Jong-un made a failed effort to reform NK's currency, which continues to repel foreign investors by levying seven types of taxes on external businesses, such as the Egyptian telecoms company Orascom which operated in the country. Ever since Kim Jong-il's son Kim Jong-un came to power, NK's experiment with partially state-controlled marketization (not quite 'free markets') has continued apace, with factories and businesses permitted for the first time to do their own accounts. In 2011, China and NK entered discussions about laying power cables from China's Jilin Province to Rason, NK. This would enable a significant degree of infrastructural modernization, in a country which frequently suffers power cuts due to its internal poverty and lack of rural infrastructure. Just one month after its fifth nuclear test, NK diplomats visited China to discuss the possibility of building hydroelectric installations.[172]

In 2015, the Pojon Responsibility System was introduced, imposing mechanization (meaning redundancy) and shrinking family farms of up to 25 workers to only 5 workers maximum. Of the returns, 75% goes to the state and, unlike in the recent past, 30% now goes to the farmers with the aim of stimulating limited forms of competition. In addition to agricultural reforms, NK has boosted its textile exports, particularly in light of sanctions which curb its mineral exports.[173]

Western – interestingly, not Eastern – oil experts reckon that NK has potential hydrocarbon deposits both onshore and offshore. Exploration by NK prospectors has begun, but no official projects have been announced.[174]

Pipeline politics: 'Peace pipelines'

This book opened with an overview of oil and geopolitics. This section is about North Korea's position within the China–Russia–South Korea energy grid. This is not to suggest that oil, gas and the geopolitics associated with them play an overarching role in US–NK relations, but rather that the proposed energy grid in the region is just one of the many factors of interest to the USA.

In 1976, China opened an oil pipeline from Dandong to Sinuiju, NK.[175]

Russia is keen to supply South Korea with oil and gas. The most feasible pipeline route would go through NK. The US is keen to keep South Korea dependent on non-Russian and non-Chinese energy. This way, South Korea is dependent on US-controlled energy imports and Russia and China lose the South Korean market.[176]

In 1990, Russia and South Korea established diplomatic relations. In 1991, Russia and South Korea signed the Vostok (East) Plan, which proposed running pipelines through NK. China's policy of energy self-reliance ended in 1993. The regional actors, including Japan, proposed constructing a Pan-Asian energy grid. Japan conducted a feasibility study of Russian energy supply lines. When the US and NK signed on to their Agreed Framework in 1994 (as the US was expanding operations in Russia's neighbour, Ukraine), Russia and China signed a memorandum of understanding to develop energy pipelines from Eastern Siberia. A formal exportation contract was signed in 1997.[177]

Of the three energy-related agreements signed in 1999, the first involved crude oil exports from Russia's Angarsk to China's Daqing region. The second involved gas exports from Irkutsk to northeast China. The third involved Siberia to Shanghai pipelines designed to take gas. British Petroleum (BP) bought a whopping 45% stake in Russian Petroleum, which helped speed up exploration. The study was completed in 2003 and planned to go on line by 2008. Shell, meanwhile, made a deal with Gazprom to make LNG swaps in the Sakhalin II project.[178]

By 2002, Japanese investors found that LNG is easier to transport by sea than building a pipeline from Sakhalin. In South Korea, President Roh Moo-hyun proposed the so-called 'peace pipelines' (which the UN supported), which would run from Russia through NK. As tensions escalated, the peace pipeline faded.[179]

Russia's gas to NK comes from or has the potential to come from Kovykta, Chayandinskoye and the offshore Sakhalin. By 2005, Russia's state-owned Gazprom continued to oppose the proposed pipeline route, fearing it would lose its monopoly. The second phase of the East Siberia pipeline would stretch to Nakhodka and bring 1 million barrels of oil per day to South Korea. It would intersect NK.[180]

South Korea sought to bypass NK by signing on to the Manzhouli II pipeline with China, which was set to involve Russia's Gazprom. However, Gazprom preferred to avoid China by building the pipeline through Nakhodka in its own territory. China wanted the Kovykta route to bypass Mongolia for geopolitical reasons. This was problematic for South Korea because SK wanted to avoid getting LGN from Guangdon and Fujian provinces.[181]

South Korea's state-owned Korea Gas Corporation decided to supply NK with liquefied natural gas instead of building pipelines. The supply of LNG to NK from the South's Korea Electric Power Corp was likely a tactic to delay pipeline construction, argued Keun-Wook Pak.[182]

Interestingly, South Korea and Russia have indicated their intent to push for NK's denuclearization only after completion of the pipelines. Dong-Ki Sung writes that Russia continues to make efforts to construct a trans-Korea pipeline, despite the fact that China's routes seem more lucrative. At the time of Sung's writing, Russia monopolized the infrastructure, such as gas pressure pumps, of the pipeline. For that reason, Russia remains keen to strike a deal on its own terms.[183]

Between 2008 and 2011, South Korea signed a Memorandum of Understanding with Russia and the leaders of both countries' major energy corporations met to discuss the project. NK meanwhile held meetings with Russia to agree on the pipeline. NK's aim, presumably, was to lessen its dependence on China and also have some political leverage over South Korea by having the capacity to disrupt gas flows to its US-allied neighbour.[184]

4

Fantasy vs. Facts

Nuclear weapons, missiles and posture: 'War could erupt from a simple miscalculation'

THAADs are Terminal High Altitude Area Defense missiles. They are not defensive weapons. Missiles are notoriously difficult to stop because missile 'defence' is like trying to hit a bullet with a bullet. The only realistic option is to destroy missile launches before they reach their top speeds and focused trajectory. Due to lack of adequate over-the-horizon radar systems, however, the given missile must at least be in its mid-course; assuming the US military is not using some secret, hi-tech system.[185]

The US is developing and stationing in Japan Aegis weaponry, Patriot Advanced Capability-3 missiles, sea-based Standard Missile-3s and X-band radars. These elements combine with THAAD to make the overall Ballistic Missile 'Defense' system.[186]

The US placement of THAAD missiles in South Korea is a problem for everyone in the region, except the US military and the Japanese establishment. For decades, Japanese citizens have resisted the US military bases in their country, as have the South Koreans. For South Korea, the THAADs are extremely dangerous because their presence gives NK added incentive to aim its missiles at South Korea. The presence of THAADs is also dangerous because China considers them, realistically, to be a threat to its national security. Russia also considers the presence of THAADs a threat.

One of the consequences of this cycle of activity is that China will strengthen its relations with NK, provoking the US to take an even harder line against the two countries. The South Korean media has been running stories balancing the pros and cons of a so-called surgical strike on NK's nuclear facilities. AN/TPY-2 X-band radars are part of THAAD. The radars are ground-based and calculate anticipated impact points of real or fake warheads from over 350 miles. They can 'see' for over 1,200 miles. Their presence in South Korea (with the pretext of deterring/countering NK) poses a serious problem for China's nuclear deterrent because it potentially enables the US to undermine China's nuclear strategic posture.[187]

NK's threats to the US island colony Guam (where NK's missiles can reach) are regularly reported in Western media. What is not reported, however, is that part of the THAAD missile system is based in Guam.[188]

Scaring the World

Other than deterring a nuclear attack on the continental USA, why does America *really* have nuclear weapons?

America's commitment to retaining weapons of mass destruction in order to provide it with operational freedoms is explained candidly in a report linked to the US State Department: 'U.S. nuclear policy remains committed to seeking reduction of global nuclear stockpiles, albeit without undermining the U.S. ability to deter any adversary and defend our allies' – in other words without having to relinquish its own weapons.[189]

In 2011, the US, France and Britain (primarily) committed grave war crimes in Libya by funding, arming, training and organizing terrorists to depose the country's dictator, Muammar Gaddafi, due to Gaddafi's refusal to open the country to US-led energy companies. The mass, illegal bombing by NATO, coupled with the slaughter of Gaddafi loyalists by the US–British-led terrorist militias, led to 50,000 Libyans dying, hundreds of thousands of refugees (including an ethnic cleansing of black Libyans by Islamic fanatics) and the disintegration of the country's political system into civil war. This was called a humanitarian intervention by the West and its bloodthirsty propagandists.[190]

In 2003, with America still reeling from the attacks of 9/11 and Iraq invaded under the pretext that it had weapons of mass destruction and links to the alleged perpetrators of 9/11, Gaddafi agreed to terminate his own weapons of mass destruction programme. This made the country even more vulnerable to full-scale invasion by the US and its allies. Indeed, one of Gaddafi's final public statements included a reference to Kim Jong-il, who had not terminated NK's WMD programme. Gaddafi said that Kim must be 'laughing' at him, as Libya was being torn apart by NATO forces. An article from NK state media read: 'In recent years, the tragedies of some countries which renounced the nuclear program half way under U.S. pressure have clearly confirmed the sensible and correct choice North Korea has made', namely keeping its alleged nukes.[191]

The US Pentagon acknowledges: 'In North Korea's view, the destruction of regimes such as Ceauşescu, Hussain, and Qadhafi [or Hussein and Gaddafi] was not an inevitable consequence of repressive governments, but rather a failure to secure the necessary capabilities to defend their respective autocratic regime's survival'.[192]

Greg Thielmann of the Arms Control Association writes

that, '[w]hen the Obama administration adjusted U.S. military doctrine to declare that nuclear weapons would only be used in response to nuclear attack, it excluded from this assurance countries such as North Korea and Iran, which were not in compliance with their nuclear Nonproliferation Treaty (NPT) obligations'.[193]

A late-2006 Congressional Research Service report states: 'Because the United States may not have the economic leverage to squeeze North Korea to collapse, it would have to try to coerce China and South Korea to discontinue their aid and economic cooperation programs that serve as a lifeline to Pyongyang'. However, the same report also notes the serious dangers involved in such a policy: 'squeezing North Korea could push it to proliferate weapons and nuclear material more quickly out of economic desperation'.[194]

US government officials are convinced that there is no hope of reconciliation with NK. This is creating a self-fulfilling prophecy, where US policymakers see NK as a hostile entity and continue to act accordingly. The Congressional Research Service report also notes the strategic irrelevance but, crucially, 'diplomatic significance' of US government officials who perceive that NK 'cannot be trusted with nuclear weapons'.[195]

A 2012 US State Department report reads: 'U.S. policymakers should recognize that Chinese perceptions of U.S. intentions, missile defenses, and nuclear and precision conventional strike capabilities will likely shape decisions about China's nuclear force posture'.[196]

Assuming NK doesn't launch a first-strike, 'the most probable cause of a major nuclear crisis in the Korean peninsula would not be war, but an unintentional nuclear incident', write two SIPRI analysts.[197]

Nukes as Defence and Diplomacy

When reporting on NK and its nuclear posture, Western media very conveniently hide the fact that, 1) the US refuses to adopt a no-first-use policy when it comes to nuclear weapons and, 2) China, Russia and North Korea each have a general no-first-use policy. When we eliminate the hot air and posturing from the equation, the cold facts are that the US could nuke any country at any time whilst the North Korean regime has pledged not to and in any case does not have the capability. According to the regime: 'we will not use nuclear weapons first unless aggressive hostile forces use nuclear weapons to invade our sovereignty'. NK has repeatedly stated that its alleged nuclear tests are designed to deter attacks from the USA, which as we have seen is committed to world domination via a policy called Full Spectrum Dominance.[198]

Other than warning the US not to escalate tensions, why is NK *really* posturing with alleged nuclear weapons? More than half of NK's alleged nuclear tests have taken place under the leadership of Kim Jong-un.[199] In 2003, the CIA confirmed that NK was seeking nuclear weapons to defend itself against US hegemony: 'A test would demonstrate to the world the North's status as a nuclear-capable state and signal (Kim Jong-il's) perception that building a nuclear stockpile will strengthen his regime's international standing and security posture'.[200]

Two researchers writing in *The Bulletin of the Atomic Scientists* say that '[t]he centrifuge facility we were shown in 2010 apparently benefited from imports from Europe, Russia, Japan, and the A. Q. Khan network prior to 2003', referring to the world's most notorious illicit nuclear materials and technology dealer, who was enabled by CIA–MI6 inaction.[201]

NK's first successful nuclear weapons test allegedly occurred in October 2006. The alleged test took place underground, making reliable seismic and radiation readings difficult to authenticate. Experts reckon that the blast was small, less than one kiloton. They 'correlated the size of the seismic disturbance with a sub-kiloton explosion, raising doubts about the effectiveness of the North Korean nuclear weapons design'. UN Security Council condemnation resulted in NK denouncing external pressure as an act of war. According to the US Congressional Research Service, possible NK motives from continuing missile launches include 'attempt[ing] to engage the United States in bilateral talks, to ensure the security of the regime, and to satisfy hardline elements within the Pyongyang government'. As well as destroying NK from within and without, one US option, says the CRS is 'withdrawal from the conflict'. But a country committed to Full Spectrum Dominance can only do that in the face of massive domestic public pressure.[202]

'[N]uclear weapons offer defense against an alliance possessing overwhelming military advantages, a source of international prestige, and a means to extort money and other benefits from neighbors', writes Doug Bandow of the Cato Institute. Bandow writes: 'For Pyongyang it would be better to seize the initiative and pre-empt the attack that it expects to come'. More likely, however, '[w]ar could easily erupt from a simple miscalculation or mistake'.[203]

In October 2006, the Congressional Research Service wrote: 'According to most informed observers, North Korea does not now have the capability to marry nuclear warheads with long-range missiles that would reach the mainland of the United States'. As we shall see, this has not changed, despite what the media claim.[204]

North Korea has yielded little information concerning precisely how it developed nuclear weapons. The authors suggest that this is a deliberate strategy. NK has modernized its uranium centrifuges and developed mobile intermediate-range ballistic missiles. Two authors writing in *The Bulletin of the Atomic Scientists* visited a nuclear reactor (Yongbyon) in NK in November 2011. They were told that the regime was building a small light-water reactor. The authors estimate that if operational, the reactor could produce enough highly-enriched uranium to make at least one bomb. But the authors were not wholly convinced that the regime was telling the truth about the operational capacity of the reactor. By 2011, NK's miniaturization efforts were still limited by its poor test record. The 2006 test was 'only partially successful'. The 2009 test allegedly yielded a 4 kiloton blast.[205]

Missiles

No NK long-range missile test between 1998 and 2009 was 'entirely successful'. By 2011, however, NK had mobile Musudan rockets with a 5,000 km range.

According to the regime, the test in October 2006 was designed 'to improve self-defence'. The test in May 2009 was 'to reinforce North Korea's nuclear deterrent for self-defence'; the test in February 2013, 'to defend the country's security . . . and in response to a hostile act the [USA]', namely the latter's criticism of NK's satellite launch; in January 2016, 'for self-defence from the nuclear threat from and blackmail by US-led hostile forces'; and September 2016, 'a demonstration to US-led hostile forces', meaning Japan and especially South Korea.[206]

Kim Jong-un's Byungjin Line commits NK to a parallel pursuit of nuclear modernization and economic growth.

SIPRI acknowledges that Kim is 'shifting the policy focus from putting military development first to also emphasizing the importance of North Korea's economic development'. But you wouldn't know it from reading or watching mainstream media, which portray Kim as a military-obsessed lunatic.[207]

A 2012 report by the RAND Corporation states that by that year, NK had only 'a few nuclear weapons available' – a speculative estimate. 'If they exist, these devices are very precious to the regime, and it seems unlikely that they would be mounted on inaccurate and unreliable missile systems – the risk of "losing" a weapon is simply too high'. The report concludes that in the unlikely event that NK would launch a nuclear missile, 'this scenario should be seen more like a terrorist attack than nuclear warfare'.[208]

James Clapper told the Senate that: 'Because of deficiencies in their conventional military forces, North Korean leaders are focused on deterrence and defense. We have long assessed that, in Pyongyang's view, its nuclear capabilities are intended for deterrence, international prestige, and coercive diplomacy'.[209]

In December 2015/January 2016, NK claimed to have successfully tested the hydrogen bomb. Many experts question the validity of this claim. White House spokesman Josh Earnest says: 'The initial analysis is not consistent with the claim the regime has made of a successful hydrogen bomb test'.[210]

In February, NK launched a satellite and in April a submarine-launched ballistic missile. A fifth nuclear test was allegedly conducted in September 2016. The government claimed that it was now capable of loading mini nuclear missiles. SIPRI refers to NK's nuclear 'deterrent', meaning that it believes that NK will not use the weapons unless it is attacked.[211]

In between its fourth and fifth nuclear tests, NK launched 20 missiles.[212]

According to NK's enemy, the Japanese Ministry of Defence (2016), NK's 'conventional forces are considerably inferior to those of [South Korea] and the U.S. Forces Korea ... It is thus speculated that North Korea is focusing its efforts on WMD and ballistic missile reinforcements in order to compensate for this shortfall'.[213]

Anthony H. Cordesman of the Center for Strategic and International Studies writes: NK 'needs nuclear weapons and missiles for both political prestige and leverage in negotiating with the United States and its neighbors'.[214]

In 2017, America's Director of National Intelligence, Daniel C. Coats, wrote, cutting and pasting from Clapper, 'We have long assessed that Pyongyang's nuclear capabilities are intended for deterrence, international prestige, and coercive diplomacy'.[215]

The threat: Image and reality: 'Deterring foreign enemies'

'While causing tremendous damage, a North Korean attack on South Korea would most likely be defeated by a U.S.–South Korean counterattack'. So write Scobell and Sanford, two analysts at the US military's Strategic Studies Institute.[216]

The Pentagon's 2012 threat assessment states that 'North Korea remains a security threat because of its willingness to undertake provocative and destabilizing behavior'. Notice that the report does not say that NK is a threat because it would actually attack the USA or threaten its population. Rather, NK is a threat because it behaves in ways not approved by the USA. This is more confirmation of the mindset of US war planners; that anyone who acts independently, even if they do not intend to materially hurt the USA, is a threat. By this standard, the USA is the biggest threat on Earth to every nation because it does not compromise.[217]

The report also acknowledges NK's 'frustration with the ROK's [South Korea] close policy coordination with the United States and its linkage of assistance to the North to progress in denuclearization'. The report gets more fascinating as we read on. NK, says the Pentagon, engages in provocative acts 'to attempt to have as equal a voice as possible in the future of the Peninsula'. So, America's real objection to NK is its unilateral efforts to strive for equality. Even more interesting is the admission that NK's militarization is part of an effort to make it 'eventually able to normalize its diplomatic relations with the Western world and pursue economic recovery and prosperity'.[218]

Ex-US State Department analyst Greg Thielmann writes (2016) that 'U.S. political commentary on North Korea vacillates between taking at face value the regime's exaggerated claims of technological prowess and reducing its leadership to cartoonish stereotypes'. Thielmann goes on to note that '[i]t is unlikely that North Korea has been able to develop a hydrogen bomb, as claimed by President Kim Jong Un', adding that NK 'is many years away from having a credible sea-based, nuclear-armed ballistic missile force'.[219]

NK's 2012 space satellite 'never stopped tumbling and was unable to carry out its announced mission'. The alleged 2015 sea-based launch of the KN-11 (Pukguksong-1) was actually 'more likely a launch ejection system test from a barge rather than a missile flight test from an actual submarine'. The as-of-2017-untested KN-08 and Musudan missiles are 'low-accuracy missiles [and] essentially weapons of terror against civilians in urban areas and [are] of limited utility against point targets or mobile military formations'.[220]

The 2016 successful satellite launch prompted some experts to suggest that the launch masked a Taepodong-2 ICBM. However, the US–Korea Institute describes the Unha space launch vehicle (or disguised ICBM) as 'highly vulnerable' and of a 'low reliability'. Thielmann goes on to write that '[s]uch characterizations exaggerate the military utility of these space launches'. Michael Elleman of the US-based International Institute of Strategic Studies writes: '[t]he accumulated experience and knowledge of past and future satellite launches will not significantly contribute to the design and development of a viable and reliable long-range ballistic missile'.[221]

Nukes

Further evidence that NK is not a real threat comes from the 2014 statement to Congress by Lt. Gen. Michael Flynn, who states that one of NK's goals is 'deterring foreign adversaries from taking actions which could threaten the regime'. Flynn goes on to imply that the South Korean and US forces in Korea could wipe out the North Koreans, writing: 'the North's military suffers from logistics shortages, largely outdated equipment, and inadequate training'. Flynn also goes on to acknowledge the low probability that NK would invade the South. 'Pyongyang likely knows that an attempt to reunify the Korean Peninsula by force would fail, and that any major attack on the South would trigger a robust counterattack'. NK's military exercises 'do little more than maintain basic competencies'.[222]

In its annual threat assessment 2015, the Pentagon says of NK that its 'nuclear weapons program [... is designed] to reinforce his regime's domestic, diplomatic, economic, and security interests'. Contrary to media claims, that NK poses a grave threat to its neighbours and the world, the report acknowledges that 'North Korea uses limited provocations – even those that are kinetic and lethal in nature, such as military actions and small-scale attacks'. The report also adds why exactly NK engages in 'limited provocations', namely 'to gain psychological advantage in diplomacy and win limited political and economic concessions', not actually threaten the US or the South.[223]

The threat assessment goes on to note that 'North Korea's national military strategy is designed to support its national security strategy by defending the Kim regime's rule and enabling the regime to conduct coercive diplomacy'. The report tacitly acknowledges that there exists a real threat against the NK regime, namely from its neighbours. 'This strategy relies heavily on deterrence, strategically through its nuclear weapons program and supporting delivery systems and conventionally by maintaining a large, heavily-armed, forward-deployed military that presents a constant threat to South Korea, especially the greater Seoul metropolitan area'. The idea that the US should de-escalate by demilitarizing in South Korea is not discussed.[224]

The report goes on to note that '[t]hese two aspects of its military strategy are meant to be mutually supporting; the threat posed by one is employed to deter an attack on the other'.[225]

Allies

One claim frequently made by Western media is that North Korea, Iran and Syria are engaged in illicit nuclear deals. A 2016 US Congressional Research Service report states:

... there is no evidence that Iran and North Korea have engaged in nuclear-related trade or cooperation with each other, although ballistic missile technology cooperation between the two is significant and meaningful, and Syria has received ballistic missiles and related technology from North Korea and Iran and also engaged in nuclear technology cooperation with North Korea.

The report goes on to say:

nonofficial assessments, including journal articles, foreign and domestic media reports, and Internet commentaries, are not always consistent with the official assessments summarized in this report. Although such unofficial sources allege a fairly significant and persistent level of cooperation among these three countries on their ballistic missile and nuclear programs, such reports lack the credibility of official assessments because they are often unsourced or attributed to anonymous government officials, frequently at odds with each other, and unverifiable.[226]

On 4 July (Independence Day in the USA) 2017, North Korea claimed that it launched a mobile intercontinental ballistic missile (ICBM) capable of hitting the USA. But is this true?

Two military experts (one with the US DoD, the other with the Dutch Defence Academy) report that the vehicle in question 'does not resemble an ICBM ... [It] clearly lacks any design margins to grow to the sort of performance that a real-purpose ICBM boasts'. If the missile carries a payload of low order of magnitude, it could exceed 5,500km but is 'not really a useful ICBM'. The model displayed by NK, the authors say, would in reality require 'covert silo basing'. NK's successful efforts to launch satellites in 2012 and 2016 are related to its long-range but not ICBM programme.[227]

North Korea's diplomacy: 'Axis of evil'

By 2008, NK had diplomatic relations with 162 out of 193 countries.[228]

Despite Western media misinformation portraying successive NK regimes as being led by hardnosed lunatics who want to provoke the US and its regional allies into war, the facts show clearly that NK has repeatedly attempted to negotiate with the USA over a host of issues. The US response is refusal, pettiness, parameter changes and insistence on preconditions. Why? The undeclared goal of the US appears to be to force the regime to collapse under the strain of US-led sanctions and successive diplomatic failures.

Greg Thielmann writes:

> The United States has sometimes reneged on its commitments, such as the timely delivery of heavy fuel oil to North Korea that it promised under the 1994 Agreed Framework. Washington has also acquiesced in South Korea's development of missiles that are not compliant with the Missile Technology Control Regime and that could target the entire territory of North Korea. Moreover, U.S. defense officials and military leaders have openly discussed the option of pre-emptive attack against North Korea.[229]

'Pre-emptive', as we know from Iraq 2003, means outright aggression in the context of US military policy.

A report by the right-wing Heritage Foundation notes that until the late '80s and early '90s, the US 'refused even casual contact with [NK] officials'.[230]

In 1990, the US claimed that it had satellite proof that NK

was developing nuclear weapons. (Around the same time, the George Bush I administration was showing the Saudis fake satellite images purporting to show an Iraqi troop build-up on the Iraq–Saudi Arabia border. The US has occupied Saudi Arabia ever since under the pretext of protecting it from an Iraqi invasion. This proves that the US has no qualms about presenting doctored satellite images to representatives.) Following the presentation of the images to the UN, the IAEA sprang surprise visits on NK, which NK rejected.[231]

Also in 1990, NK announced that it would accept IAEA inspections on the condition that the US withdraws its nuclear forces from the region. By the end of the year, the then head of the IAEA, Hans Blix, confirmed that NK was seeking assurances that the US would not attack it. The US rejected the offers.[232]

In 1992, North and South Korea signed the Joint Declaration on the Denuclearization of the Korean Peninsula.[233]

Initially, NK lived up to its agreement, halting plutonium reprocessing and eventually allowing IAEA inspectors into the country. NK even invited the USA and IAEA to inspect its reactors. The offer was rejected by a hardline Bush I administration. Writing in the respected *Arms Control Today* journal, specialist Leon V. Sigal, says:

For a country supposedly intent on obtaining nuclear weapons, that self-restraint seems difficult to explain. One possible explanation is that, starting in 1990 or 1991, North Korea was trying to trade in its weapons program for what it thought it needed more – security, political and economic ties with the United States ... Washington entered into talks only with extreme reluctance, and even then it was unwilling to specify what it would give North

Korea in return for abandoning its nuclear arms program. When it did make promises, they were not always kept, often because Washington was dependent on others to fulfill them. As a consequence, the United States very nearly stumbled into war [in 1994].[234]

Under the US–NK Agreed Framework (1994), the US was obliged to replace NK's graphite nuclear reactor with light-water plants. It never did.[235]

In 1998, NK fired a long-range missile over Japan. According to *The Bulletin of the Atomic Scientists*, this was designed in part to force the USA back to the negotiating table; a move that worked. Between 1999 and 2000, the Clinton administration re-entered talks with NK.[236]

In his state of the union address in January 2002, US President George W. Bush called North Korea part of the 'axis of evil', along with Iran and Iraq. 'Faced with such a clear and present danger', i.e., the United States, 'Pyongyang did what most countries [sic] under similar circumstances would do', namely it turned to developing weapons of mass destruction. Three scholars writing for the Woodrow Wilson Center note: '"evil" is something to be destroyed, not something to negotiate with. Indeed, the Bush administration has boxed itself – and North Korea – into a corner'.[237]

After the implementation of the Agreed Framework, the US helped establish the Korean Peninsula Energy Development Organization (KEDO). International funds were raised to transport oil to NK and 8,000 spent fuel rods from NK's Yongbyon reactor removed and sealed. The US never lived up to its obligations under the Agreement and failed to dismantle the reactors and replace them with light-water ones.[238]

In 2002, the US initiated the Proliferation Security Initiative with allies in the East China Sea, the Yellow Sea and Indian Ocean.[239]

In October 2002, US Assistant Secretary of State James Kelly claimed that NK 'confessed' to him their illicit uranium enrichment weapons programme. NK denied this. As a result of the allegations, Bush suspended heavy oil supplies delivered under the Agreed Framework.[240]

In the same year, it was alleged by the USA that NK was receiving uranium nuclear technologies from Pakistan.[241]

In January 2003, following Bush's axis of evil speech, North Korea announced its intention to withdraw from the Nuclear Non-Proliferation Treaty, which allows countries to develop nuclear technologies for civil usage, but not nuclear weapons or technologies for use in nuclear weapons programmes. The implication was that NK would begin work on developing a nuclear weapon to deter US aggression.[242]

In 2003, following the withdrawal, the US requested China take a role in mediating talks over NK's nuclear programme.[243]

The Wilson Center said that 'the prospect for another "Korean War" seems never so close as it is now'. The authors note that at the time NK signalled its intention to acquire nuclear weapons and the US threatened 'to use all means to stop this from happening'. This, the liberal authors caution, could 'grow out of all control', and emphasize (as the far-right warmonger Trump does today) China's supposed role in easing tensions.[244]

In November 2003, the US decided to halt the KEDO transports of oil to NK.

The Bush Years

Future US Defense Secretary Donald Rumsfeld (a member of the Project for the New American Century) sat on the board of the Zurich-based engineering firm ABB from 1990 to 2001, before leaving to join the Bush administration. After the Clinton administration's Agreed Framework deal with NK in 1994, it was agreed that NK could continue part of its civilian nuclear programme. ABB's chief Göran Lindahl visited NK in 1999 and even opened an office in Pyongyang before signing a light-water reactor supply deal in 2000. Bush ended diplomacy with NK not long after Rumsfeld took office. Rumsfeld's colleagues Paul Wolfowitz and Richard Armitage (two State Department diplomats and fellow PNAC members) opposed the deal with NK.[245]

Both Armitage and Wolfowitz were influenced by the neocon Paul Nitze, who replaced George Kennan in the State Department just prior to the Korean War.

In 2003, the Bush administration entered into talks with China over NK's nuclear weapons programme. NK was persuaded to attend the talks and informed both parties that the matter was between them and the USA. NK requested direct talks with the USA, but the Bush administration refused. At one of the trilateral talks mediated by China, the Bush administration made a fateful decision in rejecting NK's proposal to freeze nuclear development in exchange for economic assistance and so-called security guarantees from the USA, South Korea and Japan. The Bush administration replied that the 'military option' was 'on the table' and also 'not off the table'. This confused the Chinese- and Korean-speaking delegates, who asked, 'Then where is it now?'.[246]

The result was the establishment of Three-Party Talks.

The Talks failed for the following reasons: 1) At the first and second Joint Statement 2005, Bush prohibited US delegates from negotiating bilaterally with NK. NK responded by withdrawing from the Talks.

2) The third Joint Statement was held in collaboration with the Six Parties. South Korea agreed not to develop nuclear weapons and NK agreed for the first time to abandon its nuclear weapons programme.[247] In September 2005, the US threatened sanctions on banks doing business with NK. NK responded by boycotting the Six-Party Talks.[248] The US responded by not only slapping sanctions on NK for the first time, but also by accusing NK accounts in Macao of money laundering in support of terrorism. The US froze $25m of NK's assets and blacklisted eight NK companies. NK responded by reverting to its nuclear and ballistic missile developments.

3) At the Six-Party Talks in late-2006/early-2007, NK agreed to the Initial Actions for the Implementation of the Joint Statement. This plan outlined closing NK's nuclear facilities in Yongbyon and abandoning future programmes. In exchange, the Bush administration would remove NK from the list of state-sponsors of terrorism.[249]

Bush and Obama

In February 2007, NK's Vice Foreign Minister met in the USA with Bush officials. This was the first time that diplomacy had been so warm. One of NK's prerequisites for denuclearization was ending the US embargo. The Bush administration refused.[250]

By July 2007, the US was still freezing NK's foreign assets under spurious pretexts, but did deliver 6,200 tonnes of oil via South Korea, as agreed in the previous decade. NK permitted the arrival of the UN's International Atomic Energy Agency inspectors to verify the closing of the Yongbyon station.[251]

In September 2007, Israel and the USA brought the world

close to World War III (according to a British official speaking to the *Spectator* on the condition of anonymity), when the US authorized Israel to destroy an alleged NK-supplied nuclear reactor in Syria.[252]

By the start of 2008, US reciprocation had declined. The remaining oil promised to NK never arrived, new equipment for power plants never came and material assistance for denuclearization was not forthcoming. Despite this, NK achieved 75% unilateral denuclearization. In June 2008, NK agreed to provide reports to the USA concerning its production of plutonium. But the very moment, literally, that NK supplied the information, the Bush administration announced that it wanted an explanation of the report and failed to honour its commitment to remove NK from the list of state-sponsors of terrorism. NK reacted in kind, expelling the UN inspectors and announcing its intention to renuclearize.[253]

Also in June 2008, NK publicly demolished its Yongbyon cooling tower. The US briefly lifted sanctions but Japan refused to oblige the Six-Party agreement and supply NK with 200,000 tons of heavy oil.[254]

When US Assistant Secretary of State, Christopher Hill, visited NK and promised to remove it from the list of state-sponsors of terrorism, NK signalled willingness to reinstate the inspectors. By then, Obama had come to office and was scoring points at home by portraying NK as the bogeyman of Asia. In March 2009, two US journalists were caught operating in NK without a permit near the Chinese border and were returned by the regime to the USA. In April, NK announced its intention to launch a satellite (Kwangmyŏng-sŏng-2) and then withdrew from the Six-Party Talks, following the election in South Korea of the hardliner, Lee Myung-bak. In May, NK launched its second nuclear test. Following UN Security Council Sanctions on NK (1874), China encouraged NK to rejoin the Six-Party Talks.[255]

By January 2010, NK had agreed to a peace treaty with the USA, including denuclearization, on the condition that sanctions are removed. The US refused the offer and instead conditioned talks on the sanctions remaining in force until NK joined in the negotiations. NK's second offers on 11 January were met with ridicule by Japan. Tensions mounted again in March 2010, when a South Korean warship (*Cheonan*) exploded and sank, killing 46, as noted. NK denied responsibility but the US and South Korea immediately accused the regime of torpedoing the vessel.[256]

In April 2010, NK not only 'renewed its calls for a peace treaty' but also 'released a memorandum stating that it would limit the number of nuclear weapons it produced [and] rejoin denuclearization efforts in exchange for being recognized as a nuclear arms state'. The US rejected the offer.[257]

Denuclearization

In *The Bulletin of the Atomic Scientists* (2011), it was argued that Pyongyang 'agreed to return to the diplomatic table, its hand strengthened by advancing its nuclear program in the interim'. The authors lamented that 'Washington and Seoul remain reluctant to engage, having been burned by Pyongyang's clandestine uranium enrichment program unveiled in 2010'. In early 2011, the *Bulletin*'s authors continue, NK 'issued a barrage of statements offering to restart dialogue with South Korea'.[258]

NK was confident that issues concerning suspension of nuclearization and ballistic missile testing, as well as permitting IAEA access to sites, could be 'discussed and settled' in the context of Six-Party Talks. Then the US, France and Britain decided to illegally invade and destroy Libya, again signalling to the world that disarmament risks invasion. NK leaders met with US counterparts twice in 2011, in July and October. Nothing came of the meetings.[259]

By the end of 2011, NK expressed a willingness to resume the Six-Party Talks and held separate meetings with South Korea, Russia and the USA. But in December, Kim Jong-il died. Initially, it seemed as if Kim's successor son, Kim Jong-un, might succeed in peaceful negotiations with the USA and its allies. Bilateral US–NK talks resumed in February 2012, where NK delegates expressed their concerns that the long-standing Korean Armistice Agreement (which never actually ended the war between North, South and the USA) be concluded as a formal cessation of hostilities.[260]

The 29 February Leap Day Agreements bilaterally proposed that NK suspend nuclear and long-range missile tests and uranium enrichment. The UN's IAEA inspectors should be allowed to return. For its part, the US should cease its threatening rhetoric, provide NK with 240,000 tons of food and ease economic sanctions. The US falsely claimed that NK had violated the agreement by pursuing its satellite technology, which NK pointed out is not missile technology. After NK launched Kwangmyŏngsŏng-3 in April 2012, the US refused to deliver the food aid as promised. All the while, the regime continued feeding its people ludicrous propaganda: 'Comrade Kim Jong-il has established our motherland as an invincible political and ideological power, a nuclear nation and an unrivalled military power'.[261]

In June 2012, Obama announced that sanctions would be extended for another year. In December, NK announced the successful launch of a second Kwangmyŏngsŏng-3 satellite. The US claimed it was actually a Taeopodong-2 missile.[262]

The year 2013 went off with a bang, as NK allegedly tested a third nuclear weapon. The UN passed Security Council Resolution 2094, imposing more sanctions. In April, NK's Atomic Energy Agency announced that its Yongbyon reactor would be restarted. In May 2015, NK claimed that it had miniaturized its nuclear weapons, presumably for warfighting. In January 2016, a fourth alleged nuclear test was conducted. South Korea's President Park Geun-hye announced that the government would consider hosting US THAADs. The US military had been eager to develop THAADs as early as the 1990s, with the Project for the New American Century discussing their use in US global hegemony in September 2000.[263]

After South Korea and the US conducted the largest-ever military exercises in which they practised targeting the NK regime, NK launched five Musudan missiles. In June 2016, the US Treasury Department sanctioned Kim Jong-un's personal accounts. NK responded with more missile launches aimed at the sea. When, in August, the US and South Korea conducted their Ulchi-Freedom Guardian exercise, NK fired a ballistic sea-launched missile before conducting an alleged fifth nuclear test in September.[264]

Sanctions: 'Food aid has fallen due to sanctions'

As with Iran between 2008–14, international sanctions on NK (2006–present) have nothing to do with nuclear weapons. Rather, the real aim appears to be piling on the pressure so that the Kim regime collapses. Doug Bandow notes: 'starving the population with sanctions would be a morally dubious and likely ineffective means to transform regime personnel or policy'. Bandow argues that sanctions 'appear to have only strengthened the Kim regime's determination to develop a sizeable nuclear arsenal'.[265]

There are two significant sanctions imposed on NK: those imposed via the US-led Security Council of the United Nations (Security Council) and those imposed on US companies by the domestic House and Senate. America's Special Designated Nationals (SDN) covers NK energy, finance, labour and transport. The US also has sanctions on NK's ally, Iran. The SDN was applied to the Korea Oil Exploration Corporation when it was found to be accessing crude oil via Iran, despite the fact that the resolution does not technically prohibit this activity.[266]

UNSCR 1718 (2006) imposed an arms embargo, asset freeze and travel ban on NK, the latter specifically related to persons working on the regime's nuclear programme. The resolution excluded food and medical imports.

UNSCR 1874 (2009) expanded the above resolution to include reports by states on inspections of seizures and disposals, sales and supplies of small arms, which were not prohibited.

UNSCRs 1928 (2010), 1985 (2011) and 2050 (2012) extended the mandate of the Panel of Experts. UNSCR 2087 (2013) expanded states' rights to seize and destroy suspected materials. It also designates individuals and entities alleged to have assisted in the illicit nuclear programme.

UNSCR 2094 (2013) imposes 'targeted financial sanctions' on NK, including 'luxury goods'.

UNSCRs 2141 (2014) and 2207 (2015) extended the mandate of the Panel of Experts.

UNSCR 2270 (2016) imposes a ban on all weapons, including light ones, imposes cargo ship inspections, expands financial sanctions (including to government assets) and enforces sanctions on coal and fuel.

UNSCR 2276 (2016) extends the mandate of the Panel of Experts.

UNSCR 2321 (2016) expands 2270 above.

UNSCR 2345 (2017) extends the Panel of Experts mandate.

UNSCR 2371 (2017) imposes a 'full ban on coal, iron and iron ore', as well the exportation of seafood and the use of NK labourers in foreign countries (which means China).

UNSCR 2375 (2017) bans liquid gas to NK as well as textile exports.

The tightening of sanctions is a symptom of the worsening political situation. It also signals the cruelty of the Western powers in imposing even harsher living conditions on ordinary North Koreans, who are victims of the regime.

Between 1995 and 2006, the EU spent over 135 million euros in aid to NK. Although sanctions do not target aid, they have complex effects. Parts for tools used by aid agencies, for instance, may be affected by sanctions, so sanctions can harm humanitarian aid. There are five UN agencies operating in NK: the FAO, Fund for Population Activities, UNICEF, the WFP and the WHO. Because of sanctions, their funding fell from $72m in 2013 to $48m in 2014, despite requests for $115m.[267] In November 2016, following NK's alleged fifth nuclear test, the UN imposed sanctions (via UNSCR 2321), which put a ceiling on its coal exports.[268]

The BBC reported in mid-2017: 'The latest drought is serious, the UN's Food and Agriculture Organisation (FAO) said … because bilateral food aid to the country has dramatically fallen in recent years'. The report continues: 'This is due in part to sanctions implemented to punish North Korea over its weapons development programme. The UN's World Food Program (WFP) has also seen a steep drop in contributions'.[269]

Sanctions have banned imports/exports of copper, nickel, silver and zinc. UNSCR 2321 was drafted on China-centric terms and did little to affect trade between the two countries. UNSCR 2270, on the other hand, tightened trade sanctions but allowed China to export/import coal, iron and iron ore under so-called 'livelihood exemptions'. The limits placed on NK coal exports, however, meant that NK could export no coal exceeding 7.5 million tons per annum. UNSCR 2321 thus cut NK's national export revenue by 60%.[270]

In February 2017, China announced a freeze on NK coal imports until 2018. Its sanctions implementations have been mixed, freezing some bank transactions but not others. Diplomatically, the sanctions have added to NK's political isolation round the world. UNSCR 2321 restricts NK's diplomats and consular officials to a single bank account each.[271]

Provocations: 'We have no authority to seize cargo'
This book has documented multiple provocations over the decades against North Korea by the US and its regional allies. This section documents some more. As we have seen, the US and South Korea have been expanding their military exercises on North Korea, including plans for nuclear attacks, every decade since the 1960s.

In 1994, the US Senate adopted a resolution that President Clinton take a hard line on NK. Former President Carter was able to persuade Kim Il-sung to enter into negotiations. The *New York Times* reports that Republicans led efforts to block funding for the Framework Agreement. South Korea criticized the Republicans' move, stating: 'Any change of the accord would lead to uncontrollable instability on the Korean peninsula' (Foreign Minister, Han Sung Joo).[272]

According to a US government-sponsored study referring to 2002 (when Bush called NK part of the Axis of Evil): 'Pentagon hawks are working overtime concocting all kinds of strangulation strategies, such as [Defense Secretary] Rumsfeld's Operations Plan 5030 and the eleven-nation Proliferation Security Initiative (PSI) to establish an air and naval blockade/sanctions regime'.[273]

Displaying its commitment to international law, in this case the laws on sea searches, the US used its own and Spanish vessels to intercept a cargo ship bound from North Korea to Yemen. US intelligence claimed that the ship was carrying Scud missiles to be sold in Yemen. The US did not consult the Spanish government, prompting Defence Minister Federico Trillo to demand an apology from the US, which of course never came. Instead, White House spokesman Ari Fleischer acknowledged: 'While there is authority to stop and search, in this instance there is no clear authority to seize the shipment of Scud missiles from North Korea to Yemen. Therefore, the merchant vessel is being released'.[274]

A report sponsored by the US government published in 2011 concludes that 'South Korea, Japan, and the United States have all pulled back in their relations with Pyongyang'. South Korea and Japan means the USA, as both of those countries do as America instructs on this issue, given the heavy US military presence in both countries. This has strained China's relations with South Korea, Japan and the USA, as it finds itself excluded from the tripartite alliance over NK.[275]

In 2014, the US and South Korea began Key Resolve, joint

military exercises to which NK responded by launching missile tests.

In March 2016, the US and South Korea initiated the largest and longest-lasting military exercises (Key Resolve and Foal Eagle), which seemed to be a preparation for all-out war. They involved 300,000 South Korean troops, 17,000 US troops, battle carriers and strategic bombers. They also practised so-called decapitation strikes aimed at taking out NK's leadership and pre-emptive missile launches. NK responded by redeploying military forces and calling on reserves. It also launched five Musudan misiles.[276]

Two analysts at the Stockholm International Peace Research Institute write: 'obstacles to future multilateral talks' include the US THAAD system 'and the growth of a triangular South Korea–Japan–USA alliance among the factors reducing China's willingness to engage in US-led frameworks or talks'.[277]

America's commitment to democracy is exemplified by its stationing of THAAD missiles in South Korea in May 2017, without the knowledge or permission of South Korea's comparatively moderate President, Moon Jae-in. Reuters reports that the move coincides with 'easing tensions between South Korea and China'. The secret deployment of THAADs in South Korea was a concern for China, which reported that the weapons 'will severely damage [our] security interests and undermine the regional strategic balance'. China threatened a *de facto* blockade on SK goods in response.[278]

Conclusion: What can we do?

The events outlined in this book are serious indeed. Four nuclear-armed states – the US, China, North Korea (allegedly) and Russia – are involved in a complex geostrategic game. The US is committed to global domination at a potentially ultimate cost to its citizens, namely nuclear annihilation by war, or more likely accident. Russia, China and North Korea are seeking to defend themselves. The US is actively trying to keep NK isolated and successive governments have rejected offers of conciliation.

The likelihood of North Korea alone initiating or provoking a nuclear holocaust is extremely slight.

Compounding the research quoted earlier concerning NK's supposed nuclear-capable ICBM, missiles expert Dr Ted Postol and colleagues write: 'Western press apparently did not know one crucial fact' about NK's supposed ICBM launch on 4 July 2017 – or, didn't bother to find out. 'The rocket carried a reduced payload and, therefore, was able to reach a much higher altitude than would have been possible if it had instead carried the weight associated with the type of first-generation atomic bomb North Korea might possess'. The authors go on to note that '[e]xperts quoted by the press apparently assumed that the rocket had carried a payload large enough to simulate the weight of such an atomic bomb, in the process incorrectly assigning a near-ICBM status to a rocket that was in reality far less capable'. If the ICBM did carry a nuclear warhead, it would not be able to reach the continental USA.[279]

NK fired a second alleged ICBM. The authors write: 'in this second case, by our calculations, the second stage of the so-called ICBM carried an even smaller payload and tumbled into the atmosphere at night over the Sea of Japan'.[280]

Numerous books and articles have revealed that the world has come close on many occasions to nuclear apocalypse by accident. These include Soviet radar systems mistaking sunlight patterns for rocket launches. They include computer failures in the USA resulting in ICBM near-launches. In one case, a military vehicle was parked on top of a missile silo to prevent a launch. Nuclear madness is exacerbated by political greed and stupidity.[281]

Playing strategic power games is recognized by nuclear powers as being extremely dangerous and having a significant risk factor. Out to 2036, the UK Ministry of Defence predicts: 'Accelerating nuclear proliferation *will* create a more complex and dangerous strategic environment, with the *likely* clustering of nuclear-armed states in regions that have significant potential for instability or have fears about foreign intervention' (emphases in original). This includes the USA, which has a long-term plan to modernize its weapons systems, as do Russia and China, largely in response. The MoD report concludes: 'nuclear possession may lead to greater adventurism and irresponsible conventional and irregular behaviour, to the point of brinkmanship and misunderstanding'.[282]

Another UK MoD report on future strategic operating environments makes the chilling prediction that '[l]imited tactical nuclear exchanges in conventional conflicts … cannot be ruled out, and some non-Western states may even use such strikes as a way of limiting or de-escalating conflict'. Non-Western could easily mean Western, particularly in light

of both the US and Britain developing smaller yield warheads, including mini-nukes for warfighting in the case of the
US.[283]

People's Resistance: Japan–South Korea

Dedicated activists are putting pressure on their governments
and local authorities to de-escalate and denuclearize.

The US has 113 military bases of varying sizes and capabilities in Japan: 32 are in Okinawa alone. For decades,
ordinary Japanese civilians had engaged in dedicated protests
against the presence of US military bases, which are dangerous for a number of reasons: 1) Crashes: in 1977, Kazue
Doshida and her two children were killed when an RF-4B
Phantom II crashed near Atsugi. Crashes continue to the
present, some of which have killed US servicepeople as late as
2017. 2) The presence of young male servicemen continues to
result in rape and even death. 3) More broadly, a large US
military presence in Japan sends signals to neighbouring
countries including Russia and China that the US has no
intention of de-escalating. This only impels other countries to
adopt a tougher military position to defend against potential
US regional aggression.[284]

In 1996, following more rapes, the US agreed to relocate
Futenma air base to a less populated region. The Japanese
puppet government reneged on their promise to push for
relocation. However in 2016, after years of struggle, anti-base
assembly members won a majority in the prefectural
assembly.[285]

One anti-base activist is the 60-year-old Kumiko Onaga, a
city council member, who slept in a tent for a year opposite a
base in Henoko in the north of Okinawa. Citing pollution and
the destruction of Japan's environment by newly-built run-

ways, Onaga says: 'It's the future generations who will be greatly burdened with all the damage'.[286]

Meanwhile in South Korea, similar anti-US military protests are underway. In March 1919, two million Koreans demonstrated against the occupation of their country by Japan. Less than a century later, South Koreans are demonstrating their *de facto* occupation by US military forces, whose main target is not North Korea but China. Writing for the Fellowship of Reconciliation, Larry Kershner observes that by the end of 2014, the beautiful island of Jeju off the southern coast of South Korea, between the Yellow Sea and East China Sea, is being transformed to host 6 US Trident nuclear-armed submarines and 24 warships including Aegis destroyers. The cement used to construct the giant base has diverted water away from the UN-'protected' coral reef.[287]

In the years that South Korea was under the dictatorship of US puppets, tens of thousands of pro-democracy and communist demonstrators were slaughtered by the regimes, including over 14,000 on Jeju island. Professor Yang Yoon-mo's father and brother were killed. His mother protected him by joining the regime. But Yang rebelled and has spent his life demonstrating against the US regime and its South Korean puppet allies. 'I have become someone who is willing to die for a rock', he says of his beloved Gureombi Rock, Jeju.[288]

Activist Kathy Kelly reports on her meeting with a young married couple, Emily (who is Taiwanese) and Dongwon (South Korean) who met in Gangjeong, Jeju. 'When a barge crane was dredging the sea in front of Gureombi Rock' to build the US base, Dongwon 'climbed up to its tip and declined to come down'. He was sentenced to a year in prison.[289]

People's Resistance: USA & Europe

What can we in the West do? Aside from show our support to the South Korean and Japanese protestors, we can put pressure on our domestic governments to stop selling arms to South Korea and Japan; and indeed to the USA. We can also demand that they de-escalate the situation with North Korea by forcing America's policymaking elite to take a more inclusive, diplomatic line.

The Stockholm International Peace Research Institute says: 'Apart from their humanitarian appeal, continued exchanges between international NGOs and their counterparts in North Korea will facilitate the latter's understanding of working with the rest of the world'. SIPRI concludes that, 'these humanitarian aid networks and NGOs could become an alternative channel for communication during future potential crises'.[290]

Ex-US State Department analyst Greg Thielmann (now of the Arms Control Association) writes that the situation could be de-escalated. 'Such an outcome is feasible if the United States and South Korea are willing to ease sanctions, scale back military exercises, and negotiate a peace treaty'.[291]

In Europe, Germany's Chancellor Angela Merkel personally offered to negotiate a peace deal between the USA and North Korea: all the more remarkable considering that Germany remains occupied by dozens of US military bases and 10,000 British troops. Europe's single largest political party in terms of public membership, Britain's Labour Party under Jeremy Corbyn has urged the UN Secretary-general António Guterres to use his executive powers to force the US and North Korea to the table.[292]

In the USA, the domestic socialist Bernie 'the Bomber' Sanders (who, many would argue, is actually a New Deal democrat), initially followed the party line and indicated that escalating tensions with North Korea and China is the right thing to do. In April 2017 Sanders said that the US should be putting pressure on China to sort out North Korea, adding: 'People have been working on China for years. If Trump is doing that, he's doing the right thing'. However, when it became politically expedient to criticize Trump's North Korea policy, Sanders changed his tune.[293]

By August 2017, Sanders was saying:

> President Trump's bombastic rhetoric is not appropriate when we are dealing with the possibility of a nuclear war that could kill millions of people. North Korea's development of nuclear weapons and missile capability is an enormously serious issue and we need serious people at the State Department dealing with it. Our job now is to work with China and our allies in the region and around the world on a comprehensive diplomatic strategy to address this problem.[294]

Pew Research Center polls show that levels of public ignorance in the US are such that most Americans (particularly older Republicans) favour sanctioning NK over building closer ties. It is imperative that peace groups educate such people and pressure local political representatives, including supposed left-wingers, to take a more diplomatic approach.

It is shameful that in an age of science, supposed reason and secularization, the most dedicated peace activism is coming from religious groups.

In the US, the Pax Christi is actively supporting SPARK – Solidarity for Peace and Reunification of Korea. These groups are in turn linked to the Campaign for Nuclear Disarmament (UK) which has called for de-escalation. Matthew Bell reports that South Korean Catholics, led by Rev. Moon Kyu-hyn, are trying to find ways to defy the National Security Law, which prevents Southerners from contacting Northerners.[295]

The consequences of continued global militarization led by the US will shape the kind of unequal society that gives us a choice between far-right extremists like Donald Trump, centrist extremists like Hillary Clinton and so-called left-wingers like Bernie Sanders. Grassroots pressure on parties of all stripes is the only historically-proven method of pushing psychopathic elites to forge a saner, safer and more just world.

Notes

1. US Space Command, 'Vision for 2020', February 1997, https://ia802705.us.archive.org/10/items/pdfy-j6U3MFwlcGmC-yob/U.S.%20Space%20Command%20Vision%20For%202020.pdf. Rebecca Johnson, 'Security without weapons in space: challenges and options', United Nations Disarmament Commission, No. 3, 2003, pp. 55–6.
2. CIA, 'Middle East oil', 22 November 1960, https://www.cia.gov/library/readingroom/docs/DOC_0000010774.pdf.
3. See my *Britain's Secret Wars* (2016, Clairview Books). Michal Meidan, 'China's loans for oil: asset or liability?', Oxford Institute for Energy Studies, December 2016.
4. See my 'What Are We Doing in Afghanistan?: Surveying Euro–American Pipeline Interests', Axis of Logic, 27 October 2011, http://axisoflogic.com/artman/publish/Article_63965.shtml.
5. Zha Daojiong and Michal Meidan, 'China and the Middle East in a New Energy Landscape', Royal Institute of International Affairs, October 2015, London: Chatham House.
6. Caroline Francis, Pratheepan Madasamy, Sharif Sokkary and Sokunpanha You, 'China and the Sudan-South Sudan Oil Fee Impasse: Implications of Chinese Foreign Aid, Diplomacy, and Military Relations', Ford School, April 2012. Colum Lynch, Dan De Luce and Paul McLeary, 'The US helped birth South Sudan: Now Americans are being beaten and targeted by its troops', *Foreign Policy*, 16 August 2016.
7. *Britain's Secret Wars*, op. cit.
8. Stephanie Kleine-Ahlbrandt and Andrew Small, 'China's new dictatorship diplomacy', *NYT*, 28 January 2008.
9. Ibid.
10. Meidan, op. cit.
11. Thomas Donnelly, 'Rebuilding America's Defenses', PNAC, September 2000, https://wikispooks.com/w/images/3/37/RebuildingAmericasDefenses.pdf.

12. Ibid.
13. Ibid.
14. PSR, 'Body Count', March 2015, http://www.psr.org/assets/pdfs/body-count.pdf.
15. Hillary Clinton, 'America's Pacific Century', *Foreign Policy*, November 2011, http://www2.warwick.ac.uk/fac/soc/pais/research/researchcentres/cpd/easg/easg_calendar/america27s_pacific_century_2011.pdf.
16. Ibid.
17. Manyin et al., 'Pivot to the Pacific? The Obama Administration's "Rebalancing" Toward Asia', Congressional Research Service, 28 March 2012, Washington, DC.
18. Ibid.
19. US–China Economic and Security Commission, 'Chapter 3: Section 4 – China and North Korea', *Annual Report to Congress 2016*, Washington, DC.
20. US Department of Defense, 'The Guidelines for U.S.–Japan Defense Cooperation', 27 April 2015.
21. Shannon Tiezzi, 'China decries new US–Japan defense guidelines', *The Diplomat*, 1 May, 2015.
22. News 24, 'US rejects Russia space treaty', 12 February, 2008, and John Markoff and Andrew E. Kramer, 'U.S. and Russia differ on a treaty for cyberspace', NYT, 27 June 2009.
23. Bonnie S. Glaser, 'Pivot to Asia', CSIS, 2012.
24. US Defense Department, 'Annual Report to Congress: Military and Security Developments involving the People's Republic of China', 7 April 2015.
25. Ibid.
26. BBC News Asia Online, 'Protest as Japan paves way for self-defence law change', 15 July 2015.
27. Reuters, 'Japanese law could send soldiers abroad to fight for the first time in 70 years', 16 July 2015.
28. Manyin et al., op. cit.
29. US Council on Foreign Relations (CFR), 'Revising U.S. Grand Strategy Toward China', Council Special Report No. 72, March 2015, New York.

30. He Yun Byung-see, 'Security on the Korean Peninsula', Chatham House, 3 December 2014, London.

31. CFR, op. cit.

32. Susan V. Lawrence, 'U.S.–China Relations: An Overview of Policy Issues', Congressional Research Service, 1 August 2013, Washington, DC.

33. Manyin et al., op. cit.

34. Ibid.

35. Ibid.

36. Lawrence, op. cit.

37. Manyin et al., op. cit.

38. CRF, op. cit.

39. Ibid.

40. Doug Bandow, 'Will China Solve the North Korea Problem?', Cato Institute, 6 December 2016, No. 806, Washington, DC.

41. Bates Gill, 'China's North Korea Policy', United States Institute of Peace, July 2011, Special Report 283, Washington, DC.

42. Ibid.

43. Ibid.

44. Fei Su and Lora Saalman, 'China's engagement of North Korea: Challenges and Opportunities for Europe', SIPRI, February 2017.

45. Ibid.

46. Chen Jian, Samuel S. Kim and Hazel Smith, 'Uneasy Allies: Fifty Years of China–North Korea Relations', Woodrow Wilson Center's Asia Program, Special Report No. 115, September 2003, Washington, DC.

47. Ibid.

48. Gill, op. cit.

49. Su and Saalman, op. cit.

50. Ibid.

51. Ibid.

52. Ibid.

53. Shen Dingli, 'North Korea's Strategic Significance to China', *China Security*, Autumn 2006, pp. 19–34.

54. Ibid..

55. Gill, op. cit.

56. See my *President Trump, Inc.* (2017, Clairview Books).

57. See my *The Great Brexit Swindle* (2016, Clairview Books).

58. Manyin et al., op. cit.

59. Andrew Scobell, 'China and North Korea: Bolstering a Buffer or Hunkering Down in Northeast Asia', RAND Corporation, Testimony before the US–China Economic and Security Commission, 8 June 2017.

60. Bandow, op. cit.

61. Joe Difazio, 'Trump's Taken More Vacation Days To Date Than Obama During Presidency', *International Business Times*, 3 August 2017, http://www.ibtimes.com/trumps-taken-more-vacation-days-date-obama-during-presidency-2574250.

62. Donald J. Trump, 'Remarks by President Trump Before a Briefing on the Opioid Crisis', White House, 8 August 2017, https://www.whitehouse.gov/the-press-office/2017/08/08/remarks-president-trump-briefing-opioid-crisis.

63. *New York Times*, 'Clinton's Warning Irks North Korea', 13 July 1993, http://www.nytimes.com/1993/07/13/world/clinton-s-warning-irks-north-korea.html.

64. Harlan Ullman et al., 1996, *Shock & Awe: Achieving Rapid Dominance*, National Defense University and Institute for National Strategic Studies, http://www.dodccrp.org/files/Ullman_Shock.pdf.

65. Roberts et al. 'Mortality before and after the 2003 invasion of Iraq: cluster sample survey', *Lancet*, 2004, (364):1857–64. Reuters, 'Iraq conflict has killed a million Iraqis: survey', 30 January 2008, https://www.reuters.com/article/us-iraq-deaths-survey-idUSL3048857920080130.

66. Sean Loughlin, 'McCain praises Bush as "tested"', CNN, 31 August 2004. Even as late as 2010, the mainstream media were describing McCain as a moderate. See, for instance, Ewen MacAskill, 'John McCain swings right in desperate bid for political survival', *Guardian*, 30 April 2010. For McCain's voting record on domestic issues alone, see Jacob Weisberg, 'The closet McCain', *Slate*, 12 April 2006, http://www.slate.com/articles/news_and_politics/the_big_idea/2006/04/the_closet_mccain.html. For Trump, see my *President Trump, Inc.* (2017, Clairview Books).

67. Eli Watkins, 'John McCain: North Korea must know price for

aggression is "extinction" ', CNN, 10 September 2017. For criticism, see Adam Johnson, 'CNN Celebrates "Joy" of McCain a Day After His Genocidal Threat', FAIR, 12 September 2017.

68. Kyung Moon Hwang, *A History of Korea* (2016, Palgrave Macmillan). Ki-baek Yi, *A New History of Korea* (1984, Harvard University Press).

69. Ibid.

70. Ibid.

71. Ibid.

72. Gavan McCormack, 'Japan and North Korea: The Long and Twisted Path towards Normalcy', November 2008, WP 08-06, Research School of Pacific and Asian Studies, Australian National University.

73. Ibid.

74. Office of Secretary of Defense, 'Military and Security Developments Involving the Democratic People's Republic of Korea 2012', Washington, DC.

75. US–China Economic and Security Commission, 'Chapter 3: Section 4 – China and North Korea', Annual Report to Congress 2016, Washington, DC.

76. Jian et al., op. cit.

77. Gen. Matthew Bunker Ridgway (Ret.) *The Korean War* (1986, Da Capo Press).

78. Bruce Cumings, *The Korean War: A History* (2010, Random House). Kathryn Weathersby, 'Soviet aims in Korea and the origins of the Korean War, 1945–50: New evidence from Russian archives', Working Paper No. 8, Cold War International History Project, Woodrow Wilson Center, November 1993, Washington, DC.

79. Weathersby, op. cit.

80. Ibid.

81. Jian et al., op. cit.

82. UNSCR 84 and 85, https://documents-dds-ny.un.org/doc/ RESOLUTION/GEN/NR0/064/97/IMG/ NR006497.pdf?OpenElement.

83. Weathersby, op. cit.

84. Ibid.

85. Jian et al., op. cit.

86. Cumings, op. cit.

87. Ibid. and Bunker Ridgway, op. cit.

88. Ibid.

89. Many of the quotes were originally found in Zachary Keck, 'How American Air Power Destroyed North Korea', *National Interest*, 12 August 2017, http://nationalinterest.org/blog/the-buzz/how-american-air-power-destroyed-north-korea-21881. They have been verified and expanded upon in these sources. James Larry Taulbee, *Genocide, Mass Atrocity, and War Crimes in History: Blood and Conscience: Volume 1: Genocide and Mass Atrocity* (2017, Praeger Security International), p. 219. Michael Lind, *Vietnam, the Necessary War* (1999, The Free Press), p. 248. Blaine Harden, *The Great Leader and the Fighter Pilot* (2015, Mantle), p. 6.

90. Ibid.

91. Nuclear Threat Initiative, *North Korea Nuclear Chronology*, February 2011.

92. Jian et al., op. cit.

93. Ibid.

94. Ibid.

95. Su and Saalman, op. cit.

96. Fu Ying, 'The Korean Nuclear Issue: Past, Present, and Future: A Chinese Perspective', John L. Thornton China Center, Brookings Institution, Strategy Paper 3, May 2017.

97. McCormack, op. cit.

98. US–China Economic and Security Commission, op. cit.

99. Jian et al., op. cit.

100. Fu, op. cit.

101. Ibid.

102. Ibid.

103. Su and Saalman, op. cit.

104. McCormack, op. cit.

105. Emma Chanlett-Avery and Sharon Squassoni, 'North Korea's Nuclear Test: Motivations, Implications, and U.S. Options', Congressional Research Service, 24 October 2006, Washington, DC.

106. Su and Saalman, op. cit.

107. Ibid.

108. Ibid.

109. Chanlett-Avery and Sharon Squassoni, op. cit.
110. Maj. Daniel P. Bolger, 1991, 'Scenes from an unfinished war: Low-intensity conflict in Korea, 1966–1969', Levenworth Papers, No. 19, Washington, DC: Government Printing Office.
111. Ibid.
112. Lee Jae-Bong, 'US Deployment of Nuclear Weapons in 1950s South Korea & North Korea's Nuclear Development: Toward Denuclear-ization of the Korean Peninsula', *The Asia-Pacific Journal*, 2009, 7(8): online version.
113. Ibid.
114. Richard Helms, Director of Central Intelligence, 'North Korean intentions and capabilities with respect to South Korea', Special National Intelligence Estimate, No. 14.2-67, 21 September 1967, https://www.cia.gov/library/readingroom/docs/ DOC_0001218147.pdf.
115. Ibid.
116. Ibid.
117. Ibid.
118. NTI, op. cit.
119. Helms, op. cit.
120. Ibid.
121. Ibid.
122. Woodrow Wilson Center for Scholars, 'New Romanian Evidence on the Blue House Raid and the USS Pueblo Incident', March 2012, E-Dossier No. 5, https://www.wilsoncenter.org/sites/default/files/ NKIDP_eDossier_5_The_Blue_House_Raid_and_the_Pueblo_ Incident.pdf.
123. Ibid.
124. Ibid.
125. Stephen Wittels, 'Korean Peninsula Clashes (1955–2010)', Center for Preventive Action, November 2010.
126. North Korea and South Korea, July 4th North–South Joint Statement, 4 July 1972, http://www2.law.columbia.edu/course_00S_ L9436_001/North%20Korea%20materials/74js-en.htm.
127. Jong-dae Shin, 'DPRK Perspectives on Korean Reunification after the July 4th Joint Communiqué', Woodrow Wilson Center, 30 June 2012,

https://www.wilsoncenter.org/publication/dprk-perspectives-korean-reunification-after-the-july-4th-joint-communique.

128. Ibid.

129. Robert Collins, 'A Brief History of the US–ROK Combined Military Exercises', 38 North, 26 February 2014, http://www.38north.org/2014/02/rcollins022714/.

130. Ibid.

131. Ibid.

132. Ibid.

133. Ibid.

134. Ibid.

135. Ibid.

136. Michael Peck, 'OPLAN 5015: The Secret Plan for Destroying North Korea (and Start World War III?)', *National Interest*, 11 March 2017, http://nationalinterest.org/blog/the-buzz/oplan-5015-the-secret-plan-destroying-north-korea-start-19747.

137. CIA, 'The West Coast Korean Islands', January 1974, https://www.wilsoncenter.org/sites/default/files/2011_COHC_BB_Part_3_1974.pdf.

138. Bureau of East Asian and Pacific Affairs, 'ROKG legal memorandum on Northwest coastal incidents', US Department of State, 22 December 1973.

139. Jon Van Dyke, 'The Maritime Boundary between North & South Korea in the Yellow (West) Sea', 38 North, 29 July 2010, http://www.38north.org/2010/07/the-maritime-boundary-between-north-south-korea-in-the-yellow-west-sea/.

140. Narushige Michishita, *North Korea's Military-Diplomatic Campaigns, 1966–2008* (2009, Routledge) and Van Dyke, op. cit.

141. Ibid.

142. Van Dyke, op. cit.

143. Michishita, op. cit.

144. Gill, op. cit.

145. Mark E. Manyin and Dick K. Nanto, 'The Kaesong North–South Korean Industrial Complex', Congressional Research Service, 18 April 2011, Washington, DC.

146. Su and Saalman, op. cit.

147. McCormack, op. cit.

148. Ibid.

149. Ibid. and James Brooke, 'Japan launches spy satellite despite North Korean threats', *NYT*, 28 March 2003, http://www.nytimes.com/2003/03/28/world/japan-launches-spy-satellite-despite-north-korean-threats.html?mcubz=3.

150. McCormack, op. cit.

151. Ibid.

152. Ibid.

153. Ibid.

154. Ibid.

155. Ibid.

156. Ibid.

157. Lawrence, op. cit.

158. Harry Gelman and Norman D. Levin, 'The future of Soviet–North Korea relations', RAND Corporation, Project Air Force, October 1984, Santa Monica, CA.

159. Liudmila Zakharova, 'Russia–North Korea Economic Relations', Joint U.S.–Korea Academic Studies and *Journal of Eurasian Studies*, 2016, 7(2): 151–61.

160. Evgeny Bazhanov, 'The Russian response to the North Korean nuclear crisis: Debates and decisions', The National Council for Eurasian and East European Research, 8 November 2005, Washington, DC.

161. Zakharova, op. cit.

162. Hecker and Carlin, op. cit.

163. Siegfried S. Hecker and Robert Carlin, 'North Korea in 2011: Countdown to Kim Il-Sung's centenary', *The Bulletin of the Atomic Scientists*, 68(1): 50–60.

164. Su and Saalman, op. cit.

165. Alexander Fedorovskiy, 'Russia's Policy Toward North Korea', *Russian Analytical Digest*, July 2013, 132: 5–7.

166. Zakharova, op. cit.

167. Xander Snyder, 'Why Russia can't end the North Korea crisis', Geopolitical Futures, 26 May 2017.

168. Gill, op. cit.

169. Su and Saalman, op. cit.

170. Ibid.

171. Ibid.

172. Ibid.

173. Ibid.

174. Ibid.

175. US–China Economic and Security Commission, op. cit.

176. Keun-Wook Paik, 'Pipeline Gas Introduction to the Korean Peninsula', Chatham House, January 2005, London.

177. Ibid.

178. Ibid.

179. Ibid.

180. Ibid.

181. Ibid.

182. Ibid.

183. Dong-Ki Sung, 'Putin's Strategy on the Trans-Korean Gas Pipeline: In the Context of Pragmatic Realism', *Pacific Focus*, 28(1): 43–61.

184. Dong-Ki, op. cit.

185. Kenneth P. Werrell, 'Hitting a bullet with a bullet: A history of Ballistic Missile Defense', College of Aerospace Doctrine, Air University. Lockheed Martin, 'It really is rocket science!', 2014, http://www.lockheedmartin.co.uk/us/news/features/2014/missile-defense-stopping-bullet-with-bullet.html.

186. Su and Saalman, op. cit.

187. Fu, op. cit.

188. Ibid.

189. International Security Advisory Board, 'Report on Maintaining U.S.–China Strategic Stability', Department of State (US), 26 October 2012, Washington, DC.

190. See my *Britain's Secret Wars* (2016, Clairview Books).

191. Fu, op. cit.

192. Office of the Secretary of Defense (2012), op. cit.

193. Greg Thielmann, 'North Korea's Nuclear Threat: How to Halt Its Slow But Steady Advance', Arms Control Association, 19 February 2016, Washington, DC.

194. Chanlett-Avery and Squassoni, op. cit.

195. Ibid.

196. US Department of State, 'International Security Advisory Board Report on Maintaining U.S.–China Strategic Stability', 26 October 2012, https://www.state.gov/t/avc/isab/200297.htm.

197. Su and Saalman, op. cit.

198. Ibid.

199. Ibid.

200. Emma Chanlett-Avery and Sharon Squassoni, op. cit.

201. Hecker and Carlin, op. cit.

202. Emma Chanlett-Avery and Sharon Squassoni, op. cit.

203. Bandow, op. cit.

204. Emma Chanlett-Avery and Sharon Squassoni, op. cit.

205. Hecker and Carlin, op. cit.

206. Su and Saalman, op. cit.

207. Ibid.

208. Markus Schiller, 'Characterizing the North Korean Nuclear Missile Threat', RAND Corporation, 2012, Santa Monica, CA.

209. Clapper quoted in Anthony H. Cordesman, 'North Korean Nuclear Forces and the Threat of Weapons of Mass Destruction in Northeast Asia', CSIS, 25 July 2016 (draft version).

210. Quoted in Cordesman, op. cit.

211. Su and Saalman, op. cit.

212. Ibid.

213. Ministry of Defence (Japan), 'Chapter: Defense Policies of Countries: Section 2: Korean Peninsula', Defense of Japan (White Paper), http://www.mod.go.jp/e/publ/w_paper/pdf/2016/DOJ2016_1-2-2_web.pdf.

214. Cordesman, op. cit.

215. Daniel R. Coats, 'Statement for the Record Worldwide Threat Assessment of the US Intelligence Community', Senate Select Committee on Intelligence, 11 May 2017, Washington, DC.

216. Andrew Scobell and John M. Sanford, 'North Korea's military threat: Pyongyang's conventional forces, weapons of mass destruction, and ballistic missiles', April 2007, Strategic Studies Institute.

217. Office of the Secretary of Defense, 'Military and Security Developments Involving the Democratic People's Republic of Korea 2012', Washington, DC.

218. Office of Secretary of Defense (2012), op. cit.

219. Thielmann, op. cit.

220. Ibid.

221. Ibid.

222. Lt. Gen. Michael Flynn, 'Statement Before the Senate Armed Services Committee United States Senate', Annual Threat Assessment, Defense Intelligence Agency, 11 February 2014, Washington, DC.

223. Office of the Secretary of Defense, 'Military and Security Developments Involving the Democratic People's Republic of Korea 2015', Washington, DC.

224. Office of the Secretary of Defense (2015), op. cit.

225. Ibid.

226. Paul K. Kerr, Steven A. Hildreth and Mary Beth D. Nikitin, 'Iran–North Korea–Syria Ballistic Missile and Nuclear Cooperation', Congressional Research Service, 26 February 2016, Washington, DC.

227. Ralph Savelsberg and James Kiessling, 'Was North Korea's July 4th Surprise a Mobile Launched ICBM?', Breaking Defense, 21 July 2017, http://breakingdefense.com/2017/07/was-north-koreas-july-4th-surprise-a-mobile-launched-icbm/.

228. McCormack, op. cit.

229. Thielmann, op. cit.

230. Daryl M. Plunk, 'The Clinton nuclear deal with Pyongyang: Road map to progress or dead end street?', Asia Studies Center, Heritage Foundation, 4 November 1994, Washington, DC.

231. Fu, op. cit.

232. Nuclear Threat Initiative, North Korea Nuclear Chronology, February 2011.

233. Joint Declaration of South and North Korea on the Denuclearization of the Korean Peninsula, 1992, http://www.nti.org/media/pdfs/aptkoreanuc.pdf.

234. Leon V. Sigal, 'The North Korean Nuclear Crisis: Understanding The Failure of the "Crime-and-Punishment" Strategy', Arms Control Today, May 1997, https://www.armscontrol.org/act/1997_05/sigal.

235. Fu, op. cit.

236. Hecker and Carlin, op. cit.

237. Jian et al., op. cit.

238. Fu, op. cit.
239. Ibid.
240. McCormack, op. cit.
241. Fu, op. cit.
242. Ibid.
243. Ibid.
244. Jian et al., op. cit.
245. Randeep Ramesh, 'The two faces of Rumsfeld', *Guardian*, 9 May 2003.
246. Fu, op. cit.
247. Ibid.
248. Emma Chanlett-Avery and Sharon Squassoni, op. cit.
249. Fu, op. cit.
250. Ibid.
251. Ibid.
252. See my *Britain's Secret Wars* (2016, Clairview Books).
253. Fu, op. cit.
254. McCormack, op. cit.
255. Ibid.
256. Ibid.
257. NTI, op. cit.
258. Hecker and Carlin, op. cit.
259. Ibid.
260. Fu, op. cit.
261. Ibid.
262. Ibid.
263. Ibid. and Donnelly, op. cit.
264. Fu, op. cit.
265. Bandow, op. cit.
266. Su and Saalman, op. cit.
267. Ibid.
268. Fu, op. cit.
269. BBC, 'North Korea drought: Children at risk in "worst crisis since 2001"', 20 July 2017, http://www.bbc.co.uk/news/world-asia-40669026.
270. Su and Saalman, op. cit.
271. Ibid.

272. Steven Greenhouse, 'Republicans oppose deals with Koreans', NYT, 27 November 1994.

273. Jian, op. cit.

274. CNN, 'Spain: U.S. apologises over Scud ship', 12 December 2002.

275. Gill, op. cit.

276. Fu, op. cit.

277. Su and Saalman, op. cit.

278. Heekyong Yang and Ju-min Park, ' "Shocked" South Korea leader orders probe into U.S. THAAD additions', Reuters, 30 May 2017. Jeff Daniels, 'China renews call for Seoul to halt THAAD amid "shocking" news of new launchers', CNBC, 1 June 2017.

279. Theodore A. Postol, Markus Schiller and Robert Schmucker, 'North Korea's "not quite" ICBM can't hit the lower 48 states', *The Bulletin of the Atomic Scientists*, 11 August 2017.

280. Ibid.

281. Associated Press, 'Armored car use to block missile told' (sic), *LA Times*, 29 October 1987.

282. UK MoD, 'Strategic Trends Programme: 2007–2036', 23 February 2007 (3rd), Swindon.

283. MoD, 'Strategic Trends Programme: Future Operating Environment 2035', 14 December 2015.

284. David Vine, *Base Nation* (2015, Metropolitan Books). Okinawa Prefectural Government, 'U.S. military base issues in Okinawa', http://dc-office.org/basedata. Hana Kusumoto, 'Japanese remember mother, children killed after Marine Corps jet crashed 40 years ago', *Stars and Stripes*, 26 September 2017. CBS, 'Japan asks U.S. to finally stop military-related rapes, deaths', 23 May 2017.

285. Reuters, 'Anti-U.S. base assembly members win majority in Okinawa election', 6 June 2016.

286. Sonia Narang, 'In Okinawa, older women are on the front lines of the military base protest movement', PRI, 14 February 2017.

287. Larry Kershner, 'Pacific Pivot', FOR, 30 January 2015.

288. Kathy Kelly, 'Crosscurrents', Voices for Creative Nonviolence, 15 March 2015.

289. Kathy Kelly, 'Bowe Bergdahl and the Voice of War', Plymouth Institute for Peace Research, 10 July 2014.

290. Su and Saalman, op. cit.
291. Thielmann, op. cit.
292. Reuters, 'Trump's threat to "destroy" North Korea is wrong', 20 September 2017. *FT*, 'UK defence secretary hints at keeping troops in Germany', 1 July 2015. Channel 4, 'Jeremy Corbyn Labour conference speech in full (2017)', YouTube, 27 September 2017.
293. CNN, 'Sanders: Trump on right track with North Korea', 28 April 2017.
294. Bernie Sanders, 'Sanders statement on North Korea', Senate, 9 August 2017.
295. Independent Catholic News, 'Peace groups lobby Downing Street as US/North Korea tensions rise', 28 September 2017.

Index

ABB 81
Abe, Shinzo 14–16, 54–55
Afghanistan 4, 7, 11
Anti-Ballistic Missile Treaty (1972) 11
Armistice Agreement 50, 85
Armitage, Richard 81
Asō, Tarō 55

Bashir, Omar al- 8
Blix, Hans 78
BP 61
Burma/Myanmar 9
Bush, George H. W. 78
Bush, George W. 10, 30, 54, 78–81

Carter, Jimmy 89
Ceauşescu, Nicolae 66
Chiang Kai-shek 33, 35
China 1, 3, 5, 11–16, 31–32, 34–40, 42–48, 52, 56–65, 67, 80–81, 83, 88, 90–96
CIA 6, 25
Clapper, James 71
Clinton, Bill 10, 29, 41, 79
Clinton, Hillary 11, 52, 98
Coats, Daniel R. 72
Comprehensive Test Ban Treaty 10
Corbyn, Jeremy 96

Daesh 7, 8, 11
Djibouti 3
Donilon, Tom 18
Doshida, Kazue 94

Earnest, Josh 71

FAO 88–89
Fleischer, Ari 90
Flynn, Lt. Gen. Michael 74
France 7, 33, 35, 65, 85

Gaddafi, Muammar 66
Gazprom 62
Germany 22
Guterres, António 96

Han Sung Joo 90
Hill, Christopher 83
Hussein, Saddam 10, 66
Hyundai Asan 52

IAEA 39, 78, 82, 85
India 4, 7, 33
Iran 7, 11, 67, 75–76
Iraq 7, 10, 11, 30, 66, 78
Islamic Courts Union 8, 11
Israel 33, 83

Japan 3, 10, 12-16, 20, 24, 27, 29,

31–32, 53–56, 68, 70, 72, 79, 81

Johnson, Rebecca 6

Juche 58

Kelly, James 80
Kennan, George 36
Khrushchev, Nikita 39
Kim Dae-jung 53
Kim Il-sung 33–35, 56, 89
Kim Jong-il 54, 66, 85
Kim Jong-un 22, 29, 59, 68, 73, 85
King Kojong 32
Koizumi, Junichiro 54
Korea Gas Corporation 61–62
Korea Oil Corporation 61–62

Lee Myung-bak 51, 53, 56, 83
Lei, Hong 14
LeMay, Gen. Curtis 37
Libya 7–8, 11, 65–66
Lindahl, Göran 81

Mao Tse-tung 33, 35–39
McArthur, Gen. Douglas 36
McCain, John 30–31
Medvedev, Dmitry 57
Merkel, Angela 96
Moon Jae-in 91
Moon Kyu-hyn, Rev. 97
Mu Chong 38
Mugabe, Robert 8
Mun Se-gwang 47

NATO 7, 36, 66
Nitze, Paul 36, 81

Nuclear NPT 39–40, 67

O'Donnell, Gen. Emmett 37
Obama, Barack 11, 16, 30, 83
Orascom 60

Pak Il-yu 33, 38
Pakistan 7, 11, 33, 80
Panetta, Leon 20
Park Chung-hee 47
Park Geun-hye 86
Peace Constitution (Japan) 13–16, 49
Perino, Dana 15
Project for the New American Century 10, 80–81, 86
Putin, Vladimir, 57–58

Roh Moo-hyun 51, 54, 62
Rumsfeld, Donald 80–81, 90
Rusk, Dean 37
Russia 3, 4, 12, 14–15, 24, 32, 34, 52, 56–63, 65, 68, 85, 92

Sanders, Bernie 96
Saudi Arabia 78
Shell 62
Shin Sang-cheol 52
Six-Party Talks 21, 24, 56, 83
Somalia 8, 11
Songun 59
South Korea 3, 5, 10, 12, 13, 20, 22, 27, 36, 39, 42–65, 67, 70, 72, 78, 81, 83, 89–90
South Sudan 8
Stalin, Joseph 34–39

Sudan 8
Switzerland 22
Syngman Rhee 34, 42
Syria 11, 75–76, 83

Taiwan 24–25, 35
Tomiichi, Murayama 54
Transitional Federal Government
   (Somalia) 8
Trans-Pacific Partnership 11, 18
Trillo, Federico 90
Truman, Harry 34–37
Trump, Donald 29–30, 96–98

Ukraine 4, 61
United Nations 35–36, 46, 62
United Nations Command South
   Korea 47
UNSCR 84 35
  85 35
  1718 87
  1874 87
  1928 87
  1985 87
  2050 87
  2087 87

2094 86–87
2141 87
2207 87
2270 87–88
2276 87
2321 24, 88–89
2345 88
2371 88
2375 88
US Space Command 6
USSR 6, 34–40, 42–48

Vietnam 42–44

Wang Kon 31
Wen Jiabao 23
WHO 88
Wolfowitz, Paul 81
Workers' Party of Korea 24, 36, 38

Yang Yoon-mo 95
Yemen 11, 90
Yuk Young-soo 47

Zimbabwe 8

Books to challenge  *your perception of reality*

A message from Clairview

We are an independent publishing company with a focus on cutting-edge, non-fiction books. Our innovative list covers current affairs and politics, health, the arts, history, science and spirituality. But regardless of subject, our books have a common link: they all question conventional thinking, dogmas and received wisdom.

Despite being a small company, our list features some big names, such as Booker Prize winner Ben Okri, literary giant Gore Vidal, world leader Mikhail Gorbachev, modern artist Joseph Beuys and natural childbirth pioneer Michel Odent.

So, check out our full catalogue online at
www.clairviewbooks.com
and join our emailing list for news on new titles.

office@clairviewbooks.com

CLAIRVIEW